PENGUIN PLAYS

AFTER THE FALL

Arthur Miller (1915–2005) was born in New York City and studied at the University of Michigan. His plays include *All My Sons* (1947), *Death of a Salesman* (1949), *The Crucible* (1953), *A View from the Bridge* and *A Memory of Two Mondays* (1955), *After the Fall* (1964), *Incident at Vichy* (1964), *The Price* (1968), *The Creation of the World and Other Business* (1972), and *The American Clock* (1980). His other works include *Focus*, a novel (1945), *The Misfits*, a screenplay (1961), and the texts for *In Russia* (1969), *In the Country* (1977), and *Chinese Encounters* (1979), three books in collaboration with his wife, photographer Inge Morath. His memoirs include *Salesman in Beijing* (1984), and *Timebends*, an autobiography (1987). His short fiction includes the collection *I Don't Need You Anymore* (1967), the novella, *Homely Girl, A Life* (1995), and *Presence: Stories* (2007). His later work includes the plays *The Ride Down Mt. Morgan* (1991), *The Last Yankee* (1993), *Broken Glass* (1994), and *Mr. Peters' Connections* (1999); *Echoes Down the Corridor: Collected Essays, 1944–2000*; and *On Politics and the Art of Acting* (2001). Among numerous honors, he received the Pulitzer Prize for Drama and the John F. Kennedy Lifetime Achievement Award.

BY ARTHUR MILLER

PLAYS

The Golden Years
The Man Who Had All the Luck
All My Sons
Death of a Salesman
An Enemy of the People
The Crucible
A View from the Bridge
A Memory of Two Mondays
After the Fall
Incident at Vichy
The Price
The Creation of the World
and Other Business
The Archbishop's Ceiling
The American Clock
Playing for Time
The Ride Down Mt. Morgan
Broken Glass
Mr. Peters' Connections
Resurrection Blues
Finishing the Picture

ONE-ACT PLAYS

A View from the Bridge
(one-act version)
A Memory of Two Mondays
Fame
The Reason Why
Elegy for a Lady (in Two-Way Mirror)
Some Kind of Love Story
(in Two-Way Mirror)
I Can't Remember Anything
(in Danger: Memory!)
Clara (in Danger: Memory!)
The Last Yankee

SCREENPLAYS

The Misfits
Playing for Time
Everybody Wins
The Crucible

AUTOBIOGRAPHY

Timebends

REPORTAGE

Situation Normal
In Russia (with Inge Morath)
In the Country (with Inge Morath)
Chinese Encounters (with Inge Morath)
Salesman in Beijing

FICTION

Focus (a novel)
Jane's Blanket (a children's story)
I Don't Need You Anymore (stories)
Homely Girl, a Life
(a novella and stories)
Presence: Stories

COLLECTIONS

Arthur Miller's Collected Plays,
Volumes I and II
The Portable Arthur Miller
Arthur Miller: Collected Plays
1944–1961 (Tony Kushner, editor)
Arthur Miller: Collected Plays
1964–1982 (Tony Kushner, editor)
Arthur Miller: Collected Plays
1987–2004 (Tony Kushner, editor)

ESSAYS

The Theater Essays of Arthur Miller
(Robert Martin, editor)
Echoes Down the Corridor:
Collected Essays, 1944–2000
(Steven Centola, editor)
On Politics and the Art of Acting

VIKING CRITICAL LIBRARY EDITIONS

Death of a Salesman
(edited by Gerald Weales)
The Crucible (edited by Gerald Weales)

After the Fall
A Play in Two Acts

by Arthur Miller

Final Stage Version

PENGUIN BOOKS

PENGUIN BOOKS
Published by the Penguin Group
Penguin Group (USA) Inc., 375 Hudson Street, New York, New York 10014, U.S.A.
Penguin Group (Canada), 10 Alcorn Avenue, Toronto,
Ontario, Canada M4V 3B2 (a division of Pearson Penguin Canada Inc.)
Penguin Books Ltd, 80 Strand, London WC2R 0RL, England
Penguin Ireland, 25 St Stephen's Green, Dublin 2, Ireland (a division of Penguin Books Ltd)
Penguin Group (Australia), 250 Camberwell Road, Camberwell,
Victoria 3124, Australia (a division of Pearson Australia Group Pty Ltd)
Penguin Books India Pvt Ltd, 11 Community Centre,
Panchsheel Park, New Delhi – 110 017, India
Penguin Group (NZ), cnr Airborne and Rosedale Roads,
Albany, Auckland, New Zealand (a division of Pearson New Zealand Ltd)
Penguin Books (South Africa) (Pty) Ltd, 24 Sturdee Avenue,
Rosebank, Johannesburg 2196, South Africa

Penguin Books Ltd, Registered Offices: 80 Strand, London WC2R 0RL, England

This revised final stage version first published
in the United States of America by The Viking Press 1964
Viking Compass Edition published 1968
Reprinted 1969, 1971, 1972, 1973, 1975, 1976, 1979
Published in Penguin Books in the United States of America 1980

First published in Great Britain by
Martin Secker & Warburg 1965
Published in Penguin Books in Great Britain 1968
Reprinted 1979

LIBRARY OF CONGRESS CATALOGING IN PUBLICATION DATA
Miller, Arthur, 1915–
After the fall.
I.   Title.
[PS3525.15156A66   1980] 812'.52   78-12045
ISBN 0 14 048.162 1

Printed in the United States of America
Set in Linotype Fairfield

For my wife, Ingeborg Morath

After the Fall

Characters

QUENTIN

MAGGIE

DAN

MOTHER

LOUISE

MICKEY

LUCAS

FELICE

HOLGA

FATHER

ELSIE

LOU

CARRIE

Harley Barnes, Chairman, nurses, porter, secretary, hospital attendant, a group of boys, and passers-by

Characters

Act One

*The action takes place in the mind, thought, and memory
of Quentin. Except for one chair there is no furniture in the
conventional sense; there are no walls or substantial bound-
aries.*

*The setting consists of three levels rising to the highest at
the back, crossing in a curve from one side of the stage to the
other. Rising above it, and dominating the stage, is the
blasted stone tower of a German concentration camp. Its
wide lookout windows are like eyes which at the moment
seem blind and dark; bent reinforcing rods stick out of it like
broken tentacles.*

*On the two lower levels are sculpted areas; indeed, the
whole effect is neolithic, a lava-like, supple geography in
which, like pits and hollows found in lava, the scenes take
place. The mind has no color but its memories are brilliant
against the grayness of its landscape. When people sit they
do so on any of the abutments, ledges, or crevices. A scene
may start in a confined area, but spread or burst out onto the
entire stage, overrunning any other area.*

*People appear and disappear instantaneously, as in the
mind; but it is not necessary that they walk off the stage.
The dialogue will make clear who is "alive" at any moment
and who is in abeyance.*

*The effect, therefore, will be the surging, flitting, instan-
taneousness of a mind questing over its own surfaces and into
its depths.*

The stage is dark. Now there is a sense that some figure has moved in the farthest distance; a footstep is heard, then others. As light dimly rises, the persons in the play move in a random way up from beneath the high back platform. Some sit at once, others come farther downstage, seem to recognize each other, still others move alone and in total separateness. They are speaking toward Quentin in sibilant whispers, some angrily, some in appeal to him. Now Quentin, a man in his forties, moves out of this mass and continues down to the front of the stage. All movement ceases. Quentin addresses the Listener, who, if he could be seen, would be sitting just beyond the edge of the stage itself.

QUENTIN: Hello! God, it's good to see you again! I'm very well. I hope it wasn't too inconvenient on such short notice. Fine, I just wanted to say hello, really. Thanks. *He sits on invitation. Slight pause.* Actually, I called you on the spur of the moment this morning; I have a bit of a decision to make. You know— you mull around about something for months and all of a sudden there it is and you don't know what to do.

He sets himself to begin, looks off.

Ah . . .

Interrupted, he turns back to Listener, surprised.

I've quit the firm, didn't I write you about that? Really! I was sure I'd written. Oh, about fourteen months ago; a few weeks after Maggie died. *Maggie stirs on the second platform.* It just got to where I couldn't concentrate on a case any more; not the way I used to. I felt I was merely in the service of my own success. It all lost any point. Although I do wonder sometimes if I am simply trying to destroy myself. . . . Well, I have walked away from what passes for an important career. . . . Not very much, I'm afraid; I still live in the hotel, see a few people, read a good deal— *Smiles*—stare out the window. I don't know why I'm smiling; maybe I feel that's all over now, and I'll harness myself to something again. Although I've had that feeling before and done nothing about it, I—

Again, interrupted, he looks surprised.

God, I wrote you about *that*, didn't I? Maybe I dream these letters. Mother died. Oh, it's four—*Airplane sound is heard behind him*—five months ago now. Yes, quite suddenly; I was in Germany at the time and—it's one of the things I wanted—*Holga appears on upper platform, looking about for him*—to talk to you about. I . . . met a woman there. *He grins.* I never thought it could happen again, but we became quite close. In fact, she's arriving tonight, for some conference at Columbia—she's an archaeologist. I'm not sure, you see, if I want to lose her, and yet it's outrageous to think of committing myself again. . . . Well, yes, but look at my life. A life, after all, is evidence, and I have two divorces in my safe-deposit box. *Turning to glance up at Holga*: I tell you frankly, I'm a little afraid. . . . Well, of who and what I'm bringing to her. *He sits again, leans forward.* You know, more and more I think that for many years I looked at life like a case at law, a series of proofs. When you're young you prove how brave you are, or smart; then, what a good lover; then, a good father; finally, how wise, or powerful or what-the-hell-ever. But underlying it all, I see now, there was a presumption. That I was moving on an upward path toward some elevation, where—God knows what—I would be justified, or even condemned—a verdict anyway. I think now that my disaster really began when I looked up one day—and the bench was empty. No judge in sight. And all that remained was the endless argument with oneself—this pointless litigation of existence before an empty bench. Which, of course, is another way of saying—despair. And, of course, despair can be a way of life; but you have to believe in it, pick it up, take it to heart, and move on again. Instead, I seem to be hung up. *Slight pause.* And the days and the months and now the years are draining away. A couple of weeks ago I suddenly became aware of a strange fact. With all this darkness, the truth is that every morning when I awake, I'm full of hope!

With everything I know—I open my eyes, I'm like a boy! For an instant there's some—unformed promise in the air. I jump out of bed, I shave, I can't wait to finish breakfast—and then, it seeps in my room, my life and its pointlessness. And I thought —if I could corner that hope, find what it consists of and either kill it for a lie, or really make it mine . . .

FELICE, *having entered*: You do remember me, don't you? Two years ago in your office, when you got my husband to sign the divorce papers?

QUENTIN, *to Listener*: I'm not sure why I bring her up. I ran into her on the street last month . . .

FELICE: I always wanted to tell you this—you changed my life!

QUENTIN, *to Listener*: There's something about that girl unnerves me.

FELICE, *facing front, standing beside him*: You see, my husband was always so childish, alone with me. But the way you talked to him; it made him act so dignified I almost began to love him! And when we got out in the street he asked me something. Should I tell you, or do you know already?

QUENTIN, *now turning to her*: He asked to go to bed with you one last time?

FELICE: How did you know that?

QUENTIN: Well, what harm would it have done?

FELICE: But wouldn't it be funny the same day we agreed to divorce?

QUENTIN: Honey, you never stop loving whoever you loved. Why must you try?

> *Louise starts down toward him, and Maggie appears far upstage in gold dress among anonymous men. Quentin turns back to Listener.*

Why do I make such stupid statements!

MAGGIE, *from among the men, laughing as though with joy at seeing him*: Quentin! *She is gone.*

QUENTIN: These goddamned women have injured me! Have I learned nothing?

HOLGA, *appearing under the tower with flowers as Maggie and men go dark*: Would you like to see Salzburg? I think they play *The Magic Flute* tonight.

QUENTIN, *of Holga*: I don't know what I'd be bringing to that girl.

> *Holga exits. Louise has moved down in front of him, and he glances at her.*

I don't know how to blame with confidence.

FELICE, *as Louise moves thoughtfully upstage and exits*: But I finally got your point! It's that there is no point, right? No one has to be to blame! And as soon as I realized that, I started to dance better!

QUENTIN, *to Listener*: God, what excellent advice I give!

FELICE: I almost feel free when I dance now! Sometimes I only have to think high and I go high! I get a long thought and I fly across the floor. *She flies out into darkness.*

QUENTIN: And on top of that she came back again the other night, flew into my room—reborn! She made me wonder how much I believe in life.

FELICE, *rushing on*: I had my nose fixed! Could I show it to you? The doctor took the bandage off, but I put it back because I wanted you to be the first! Do you mind?

QUENTIN, *turning to her*: No. But why me?

FELICE: Because—remember that night I came up here? I was trying to decide if I should have it done. 'Cause there could be something insincere about changing your nose; I wouldn't want to build everything on the shape of a piece of cartilage. You don't absolutely have to answer me, but—I think you wanted to make love to me that night. Didn't you?

QUENTIN: I did, yes.

FELICE: I knew it! And I felt it didn't matter what kind of nose I had! So I might as well have a short one! Could I show it to you?

QUENTIN: I'd like very much to see it.

FELICE: Close your eyes. *He does. She lifts the bandage.* Okay. *He looks. She raises her arm in blessing.* I'll always bless you. Always!

He slowly turns to the Listener as she walks into darkness.

QUENTIN: And I even liked her first nose better. And yet I may stand in her mind like some important corner she turned in life. And she meant so little to me. I feel like a mirror in which she somehow saw herself as glorious.

Two pallbearers in the distance carry an invisible coffin.

It's like my mother's funeral;

Mother appears on upper platform, arms crossed as in death.

I still hear her voice in the street sometimes, loud and real, calling me. And yet she's under the ground. That whole cemetery—I saw it like a field of buried mirrors in which the living merely saw themselves. I don't seem to know how to grieve for her.

Father appears, a blanket over him; two nurses tend him.

Or maybe I don't believe that grief is grief unless it kills you.

Dan appears, talking to a nurse.

Like when I flew back and met my brother in the hospital.

The nurse hurries out, and Quentin has gotten up and moved to Dan.

DAN: I'm so glad you got here, kid; I wouldn't have wired you, but I don't know what to do. You have a good flight?

QUENTIN, *to Dan*: But what's the alternative? She's dead, he has to know.

DAN, *to Quentin*: But he was only operated on this morning. How can we walk in and say, "Your wife is dead"? It's like sawing off his arm. Suppose we tell him she's on her way, then give him a sedative?

QUENTIN: But Dan, don't you think it belongs to him? After fifty years you owe one another a death.

DAN: Kid, the woman was his right hand; without her he was never very much, you know—he'll fall apart.

QUENTIN: I can't agree; I think he's got a lot of stuff—*Without halt, to the Listener*: Which is hilarious! . . . Because! He was always the one who idolized the old man, and I saw through him from the beginning! Suddenly we're changing places, like children in a game! I don't know any more what people *are* to one another!

DAN, *as though he had come to a decision*: All right; let's go in, then.

QUENTIN: You want me to tell him?

DAN, *unwillingly, afraid but challenged*: I'll do it.

QUENTIN: I could do it, Dan. It belongs to him, as much as his wedding.

DAN, *relieved*: All right, if you don't mind.

They turn together toward Father in the bed. He does not see them yet. They move with the weight of their news. Quentin turns toward Listener as he walks.

QUENTIN: Or is it simply that I am crueler than he?

Now Father sees them and raises up his arm.

DAN, *indicating Quentin*: Dad, look . . .

FATHER: For cryin' out loud! Look who's here! I thought you were in Europe!

QUENTIN: Just got back. How are you?

DAN: You look wonderful, Dad.

FATHER: What do you mean, "look"? I *am* wonderful! I tell you, I'm ready to go through it again! *They laugh proudly with him.* I mean it—the way that doctor worries, I finally told him, "Look, if it makes you feel so bad you lay down and I'll operate!" Very fine man. I thought you'd be away couple months more.

QUENTIN, *hesitantly*: I decided to come back and—

DAN, *breaking in, his voice turning strange*: Sylvia'll be right in. She's downstairs buying you something.

FATHER: Oh, that's nice! I tell you something, fellas—that kid is more and more like Mother. Been here every day . . . Where is Mother? I been calling the house.

The slightest empty, empty pause.

DAN: One second, Dad, I just want to—

Crazily, without evident point, he starts calling, and moving upstage toward the nurse. Quentin is staring at his father.

Nurse! Ah . . . could you call down to the gift shop and see if my sister . . .

FATHER: Dan! Tell her to get some ice. When Mother comes you'll all have a drink! I got a bottle of rye in the closet. *To Quentin*: I tell you, kid, I'm going to be young. Mother's right; just because I got old I don't have to act old. I mean we could go to Florida, we could—

QUENTIN: Dad.

FATHER: What? Is that a new suit?

QUENTIN: No, I've had it.

FATHER, *remembering—to Dan, of the nurse*: Oh, tell her glasses, we'll need more glasses.

QUENTIN: Listen, Dad.

Dan halts and turns back.

FATHER, *totally unaware, smiling at his returned son*: Yeah?

QUENTIN: Mother died. She had a heart attack last night on her way home.

FATHER: Oh, no, no, no, no.

QUENTIN: We didn't want to tell you but—

FATHER: Ahhh! Ahhh, no, no, no.

DAN: There's nothing anybody could have done, Dad.

FATHER: Oh. Oh. Oh!

QUENTIN, *grasping his hand*: Now look, Dad, you're going to be all right, you'll—

FATHER—*it is all turning into a deep gasping for breath*: Oh boy. Oh boy! No, no.

DAN: Now look, Dad, you're a hell of a fella. Dad, listen—

FATHER: Goddammit! I couldn't take care of myself, I knew she was working too hard!

QUENTIN: Dad, it's not your fault, that can happen to anyone—

FATHER: But she was sitting right here. She was—she was right here!

QUENTIN: Pa . . . Pa . . .

Dan moves in close, as though to share him.

FATHER: Oh, boys—she was my right hand! *He raises his fist and seems about to lose his control again.*

DAN: We'll take care of you, Dad. I don't want you to worry about—

FATHER: No-no. I'll be all right. God! Now I'm better! Now, *now* I'm better!

> *They are silent.*

So where is she?

QUENTIN: In the funeral parlor.

FATHER, *shaking his head—an explosive blow of air:* Paaaaaah!

QUENTIN: We didn't want to tell you but we figured you'd rather know.

FATHER: Ya. Thanks. Thanks. I'll . . . *He looks up at Quentin.* I'll just have to be stronger.

QUENTIN: That's right, Dad.

FATHER, *to no one, as Mother disappears above:* This . . . will make me stronger. *But the weeping threatens; he clenches his jaw, shakes his head, and indicates a point.* She was right here!

> *He is taken away by the nurses and Dan. Quentin comes slowly to the Listener.*

QUENTIN: Still and all, a couple months later he bothered to register and vote. . . . Well, I mean . . . it didn't kill him either, with all his tears. I don't know what the hell I'm driving at. It's connected to . . .

> *The tower gradually begins to light. He is caught by it.*

I visited a concentration camp in Germany.

> *He has started toward the tower when Felice appears, raising her arm in blessing.*

FELICE: Close your eyes, okay?

QUENTIN, *turned by her force*: I don't understand why that girl sticks in my mind. *He moves toward her now.* She did, she offered me some . . . love, I guess. And if I don't return it—it's like owing for a gift that you didn't ask for.

Mother has appeared again; she raises her hand in blessing as Felice does.

FELICE: I'll always bless you!

She exits and Mother is gone.

QUENTIN: When she left . . . I did a stupid thing. I don't understand it. There are two light fixtures on the wall of my hotel room . . .

As he speaks Maggie enters onto second platform, dressed in negligee, hair disheveled. Quentin struggles against his own disgust.

I noticed for the first time that they're . . . a curious distance apart. And I suddenly saw that if you stood between them—*He spreads out his arms*—you could reach out and rest your arms.

Just before he completely spreads his arms, Maggie sits up, her breathing sounds.

MAGGIE: Liar! Judge!

He drops his arms, aborting the image; Maggie exits.

Now Holga appears and is bending to read a legend fixed to the wall of a torture chamber.

QUENTIN: Oh. The concentration camp . . . this woman . . . Holga took me there.

HOLGA, *turning to "him," as though he stood beside her*: This is the room where they tortured them. No, I don't mind, I'll translate it.

She returns to the legend; he slowly approaches behind her.

"The door to the left leads into the chamber where their teeth were extracted for gold; the drain in the floor carried off the blood. At times, instead of shooting, they were individually strangled to death. The barracks on the right were the bordello where women—"

QUENTIN: I think you've had enough, Holga.

HOLGA: No, if you want to see the rest—

QUENTIN, *taking her arm*: Let's walk, dear. Country looks lovely out there.

They walk. The light changes to day.

They sure built solid watchtowers, didn't they! Here, this grass looks dry; let's sit down.

They sit. Pause.

I always thought the Danube was blue.

HOLGA: Only the waltz; although it does change near Vienna, out of some lingering respect for Strauss, I suppose.

QUENTIN: I don't know why this hit me so.

HOLGA: I'm sorry! *Starting to rise as she senses an estrangement— to raise his spirits*: You still want to see Salzburg? I'd love to show you Mozart's house. And the cafés are excellent there.

QUENTIN, *turning to her now*: Was there somebody you knew died here?

HOLGA: Oh no. I feel people ought to see it, that's all. And you seemed so interested.

QUENTIN: Yes, but I'm an American. I can afford to be interested.

HOLGA: Don't be too sure. When I first visited America after the war I was three days under questioning before they let me in.

How could one be in forced labor for two years if one were not a Communist or a Jew? In fact, it was only when I told them I had blood relatives in several Nazi ministries that they were reassured. It's as though fifteen years of one's life had simply vanished in some insane confusion. So I was very glad you were so interested.

QUENTIN, *glancing up at the tower*: I guess I thought I'd be indignant, or angry. But it's like swallowing a lump of earth. It's strange.

HOLGA, *pressing him to lie down, cheerfully*: Come, lie down here for a while and perhaps—

QUENTIN: No, I'm—*He has fended off her hand.* I'm sorry, dear, I didn't mean to push you away.

HOLGA, *rebuffed and embarrassed*: I see wildflowers on that hill; I'll pick some for the car! *She gets up quickly.*

QUENTIN: Holga? *She continues off. He jumps up and hurries to her, turning her.* Holga. *He does not know what to say.*

HOLGA: Perhaps we've been together too much. I could rent another car at Linz; we could meet in Vienna sometime.

QUENTIN: I don't want to lose you, Holga.

HOLGA: I hear your wings opening, Quentin. I am not helpless alone. I love my work. It's simply that from the moment you spoke to me I felt somehow familiar, and it was never so before. . . . It isn't a question of getting married; I am not ashamed this way. But I must have *something*.

QUENTIN: I don't give you anything?

HOLGA: You give me very much. . . . It's difficult for me to speak like this. I am not a woman who must be reassured every minute, those women are stupid to me. . . .

QUENTIN, *turning her face to him*: Holga, are you weeping—for *me*?

HOLGA: Yes.

QUENTIN: It's that I don't want to abuse your feeling for me—I swear I don't know if I have lived in good faith. And the doubt ties my tongue when I think of promising anything again.

HOLGA: But how can one ever be sure of one's good faith?

QUENTIN, *surprised*: God, it's wonderful to hear you say that. All my women have been so goddamned sure!

HOLGA: But how can one ever be?

QUENTIN—*he kisses her gratefully*: Why do you keep coming back to this place? It seems to tear you apart.

> *Mother is heard softly singing a musical comedy ballad of the twenties.*

HOLGA, *after a pause; she is disturbed, uncertain*: I . . . don't know. Perhaps . . . because I didn't die here.

QUENTIN, *turning quickly to Listener*: What?

HOLGA: Although that would make no sense! I don't really know!

QUENTIN, *going toward the Listener at the edge of the stage*: That people . . . what? "Wish to die for the dead." No-no, I can understand it; survival can be hard to bear. But I—I don't think I feel that way. . . . Although I do think of my mother now, and she's dead. Yes! *He turns to Holga.* And maybe the dead do bother her.

HOLGA: It was the middle of the war. I had just come out of a class and there were British leaflets on the sidewalk. And photographs of a concentration camp. And emaciated people. One tended to believe the British. I'd had no idea. Truly. It isn't easy to turn against your country; not in a war. Do Americans turn against America because of Hiroshima? There are reasons always. And I took the leaflet to my godfather—he was still commanding our Intelligence. And I asked if it were true. "Of course," he said, "why does it excite you?" And I said, "You are a swine. You are all swine." I threw my briefcase at him. And he opened it and put some papers in it and asked me to deliver it to a certain address. And I became a courier for the officers who were planning to assassinate Hitler. . . . They were all hanged.

QUENTIN: Why not you?

HOLGA: They didn't betray me.

QUENTIN: Then why do you say good faith is never sure?

HOLGA, *after a pause*: It was my country—longer, perhaps, than it should have been. But I didn't know. And now I don't know how I could not have known.

QUENTIN: Holga, I bless your uncertainty. You don't seem to be looking for some goddamned . . . moral *victory*. Forgive me, I didn't mean to be distant with you. I—*Looks up.*

HOLGA: I'll get the flowers! *She starts away.*

QUENTIN: It's only this place!

HOLGA, *turning, and with great love*: I know! I'll be right back! *She hurries away.*

> He stands in stillness a moment; the presence of the tower bores in on him; its color changes; he now looks up at it and addresses the Listener.

QUENTIN: I think I expected it to be more unfamiliar. I never thought the stones would look so ordinary. And the view from here is rather pastoral. Why do I *know* something here? Even hollow now and empty, it has a face, and asks a sort of question: "What do you believe as true as this?" Yes! Believers built this, maybe that's the fright—and I, without belief, stand here disarmed. I can see the convoys grinding up this hill, and I inside; no one knows my name and yet they'll smash my head on a concrete floor! And no appeal . . . *He turns quickly to the*

Listener. Yes! It's that I no longer see some final saving grace! Socialism once, then love; some final hope is gone that always saved before the end!

Mother appears; Dan enters, kisses her, and exits.

MOTHER, *to an invisible small boy*: Not too much cake, darling, there'll be a lot of food at this wedding.

QUENTIN: Mother! That's strange. And murder?

MOTHER, *getting down on her knees to tend the little boy*: Yes, garters, Quentin, and don't argue with me. . . . Because it's my brother's wedding and your stockings are not to hang over your shoes!

QUENTIN—*he has started to laugh but it turns into*: Why can't I mourn her? And Holga wept in there, why can't I weep? Why do I feel an understanding with this slaughterhouse?

Mother laughs. He turns to her

MOTHER, *to the little boy*: My brothers! Why must every wedding in this family be a catastrophe! . . . Because the girl is pregnant, darling, and she's got no money, she's stupid, and I tell you this one is going to end up with a mustache! That's why, darling, when you grow up, I hope you learn how to disappoint people. Especially women.

QUENTIN, *watching her, sitting nearby*: But what the hell has this got to do with a concentration camp?

MOTHER: Will you stop playing with matches? *Slaps an invisible boy's hand.* You'll pee in bed! Why don't you practice your penmanship instead? You write like a monkey, darling. And where is your father? If he went to sleep in the Turkish bath again,. I'll kill him! Like he forgot my brother Herbert's wedding and goes to the Dempsey-Tunney fight. And ends up in the men's room with the door stuck, so by the time they get him out my brother's married, there's a new champion, and it cost him a hundred dollars to go to the men's room! *She is laughing.*

Father with secretary has appeared on upper platform, an invisible phone to his ear.

FATHER: Then cable Southampton.

MOTHER: But you mustn't laugh at him, he's a wonderful man.

FATHER: Sixty thousand tons. Sixty.

Father disappears.

MOTHER: To this day he walks into a room you want to bow! *Warmly*: Any restaurant—one look at him and the waiters start moving tables around. *Because*, dear, people know that this is a *man*. Even Doctor Strauss, at my wedding he came over to me, says, "Rose, I can see it looking at him, you've got a wonderful man," and he was always in love with me, Strauss. . . . Oh, sure, but he was only a penniless medical student then, my father wouldn't let him in the house. Who knew he'd end up so big in the gallstones? That poor boy! Used to bring me novels to read, poetry, philosophy, God knows what! One time we even sneaked off to hear Rachmaninoff together. *She laughs sadly; and with wonder more than bitterness.* That's why, you see, two weeks after we were married; sit down to dinner and Papa hands me a menu and asks me to read it to him. Couldn't *read! I* got so frightened I nearly ran away! . . . Why? Because your grandmother is such a fine, unselfish woman; two months in school and they put him into the shop! That's what some women are, my dear—and now he goes and buys her a new Packard every year. *With a strange and deep fear*: Please, darling, I want you to *draw* the letters, that scribbling is ugly, dear; and your posture, your speech, it can all be beautiful! Ask Miss Fisher, for years they kept my handwriting pinned up on the bulletin board; God, I'll never forget it, valedictorian of the class with a scholarship to Hunter in my hand . . . *A blackness flows into her soul.* And I came home, and Grandpa says, "You're getting married!" I was like—like with small wings, just getting ready to fly; I slept all year with the catalogue under my pillow. To learn, to learn everything! Oh, darling, the whole thing is such a mystery!

Father enters the area, talking to the young, invisible Quentin.

FATHER: Quentin, would you get the office on the phone? *To Mother*: Why would you call the Turkish bath?

MOTHER: I thought you forgot about the wedding.

FATHER: I wish I could, but I'm paying for it.

MOTHER: He'll pay you back!

FATHER: I believe it, I just wouldn't want to hang by my hair that long. *He turns, and, going to a point, he takes up an invisible phone.* Herman? Hold the wire.

MOTHER: I don't want to be late, now.

FATHER: She won't give birth if we're half-hour late.

MOTHER: Don't be so smart! He fell in love, what's so terrible about that?

FATHER: They all fall in love on my money. I married into a love nest! *He turns to Quentin, laughing.* Did they pass a law that kid can't get a haircut? *Reaching into his pocket, tossing a coin*: Here, at least get a shine. *To Mother*: I'll be right up, dear, go ahead.

MOTHER: I'll put in your studs. God, he's so beautiful in a tuxedo!

She goes a distance out of the area, but halts, turns, eavesdrops on Father.

FATHER, *into phone*: Herman? The accountant still there? Put him on.

QUENTIN, *suddenly, recalling, to the Listener*: Oh, yes!

FATHER: Billy? You finished? Well, what's the story, where am I?

QUENTIN: Yes!

· 18 ·

FATHER: Don't you read the papers? What'll I do with Irving Trust? I can't give it away. What bank?

Mother descends a step, alarmed.

I been to every bank in New York, I can't get a bill paid, how the hell they going to lend me money? No-no, there's no money in London, there's no money in Hamburg, there's no money in London, there's no money in Hamburg, there's no money in the world, the ocean's empty, Billy—now tell me the truth, where am I?

He puts down the phone. Pause. Mother comes up behind him. He stands almost stiffly, as though to take a storm.

MOTHER: What's that about? What are you winding up?

Father stands staring; but she seems to hear additional shocking facts.

What are you talking about? When did this start? . . . Well, how much are you taking out of it? . . . You lost your mind? You've got over four hundred thousand dollars' worth of stocks, you can sell the—

Father laughs silently.

You sold those wonderful stocks? I just bought a new grand piano, why didn't you say something? And a silver service for my brother, and you don't say anything! *More subdued, she walks a few steps in thought.* Well, then—you'd better cash your insurance; you've got at least seventy-five thousand cash value—*Halts, turning in shock.* When!

Father is gradually losing his stance, his grandeur; he pulls his tie loose.

All right, then—we'll get rid of my bonds. Do it tomorrow. . . . What do you mean? Well, you get them back, I've got ninety-one thousand dollars in bonds you gave me. Those are my bonds. I've got bonds—*She breaks off, open horror on her face and now a growing contempt.* You mean you saw everything going down and you throw good money after bad? Are you some kind of a moron?

FATHER: You don't walk away from a business; I came to this country with a tag around my neck like a package in the bottom of the boat!

MOTHER: I should have run the day I met you.

FATHER, *as though stabbed*: Rose! *He sits, closing his eyes, his neck bent.*

MOTHER: I should have done what my sisters did, tell my parents to go to hell and thought of myself for once! I should have run for my life!

FATHER, *indicating a point nearby*: Sssh, I hear the kids—

MOTHER: I ought to get a divorce!

FATHER: Rose, the college men are jumping out of windows.

MOTHER: But your last dollar! *Bending over, into his face*: You are an idiot!

Her nearness forces him to stand; they look at each other, strangers.

QUENTIN, *looking up at the tower*: Yes! For no reason—they don't even ask your name!

FATHER, *looking toward the nearby point*: Somebody crying? Quentin's in there. You better talk to him.

She goes in some trepidation toward the indicated point. A foot or so from it, she halts.

MOTHER: Quentin? Darling? You better get dressed. Don't cry, dear—

She is stopped short by something "Quentin" has said.

What *I* said? Why, what did I say? . . . Well, I was a little angry, that's all, but I never said *that*. I think he's a wonderful man! *Laughs.* How could I say a thing like that? Quentin! *As though he is disappearing, she extends her arms.* I didn't say anything! *With a cry toward someone lost, rushing out after the boy:* Darling, I didn't say anything!

Father and Dan exit.

Instantly Holga appears, coming toward him.

QUENTIN, *to himself, turning up toward the tower:* They don't even ask your name.

HOLGA, *looking about for him:* Quentin? Quentin?

QUENTIN, *to Holga:* You love me, don't you?

HOLGA: Yes. *Of the wildflowers in her arms:* Look, the car will be all sweet inside!

QUENTIN, *clasping her hands:* Let's get out of this dump. Come on, I'll race you to the car!

HOLGA: Okay! On your mark!

They get set.

QUENTIN: Last one there's a rancid wurst!

HOLGA: Get ready! Set!

Quentin suddenly looks up at the tower and sits on the ground as though he had committed a sacrilege.

She has read his emotion, touches his face.

Quentin, dear—no one they didn't kill can be innocent again.

QUENTIN: But how did you solve it? How do you get so purposeful? You're so full of hope!

HOLGA: Quentin, I think it's a mistake to ever look for hope outside one's self. One day the house smells of fresh bread, the next of smoke and blood. One day you faint because the gardener cut his finger off, within a week you're climbing over the corpses of children bombed in a subway. What hope can there be if that is so? I tried to die near the end of the war. *She rises, moves up the stair toward the tower.* The same dream returned each night until I dared not go to sleep and grew quite ill. I dreamed I had a child, and even in the dream I saw it was my life, and it was an idiot, and I ran away. But it always crept onto my lap again, clutched at my clothes. Until I thought, if I could kiss it, whatever in it was my own, perhaps I could sleep. And I bent to its broken face, and it was horrible . . . but I kissed it. I think one must finally take one's life in one's arms, Quentin. Come, they play *The Magic Flute* tonight. You like *The Magic Flute?*

She exits from beneath the tower on the upper level.

QUENTIN, *alone:* I miss her . . . badly. And yet, I can't sign my letters to her "With love." I put, "Sincerely," or "As ever"—*Felice enters far away upstage*—some such brilliant evasion. I've lost the sense of some absolute necessity. Whether I open a book or think of marrying again, it's so damned clear I'm choosing what I do—and it cuts the strings between my hands and heaven. It sounds foolish, but I feel . . . unblessed.

Felice holds up her hand in blessing, then exits.

And I keep looking back to when there seemed to be some duty in the sky. I had a dinner table and a wife—*In the distance Louise appears with a dishcloth, wiping silver, wearing a kitchen apron*—a child and the world so wonderfully threatened by injustices I was born to correct! It seems so fine! Remember—when there were good people and bad people? And how easy it was to tell! The worst son of a bitch, if he loved Jews and hated Hitler, he was a buddy. Like some kind of paradise compared to this.

He is aware of Elsie appearing on second platform; a beach robe hangs from her shoulders, her arms out of the sleeves, her back to us.

· 22 ·

Until I begin to look at it. God, when I think of what I believed I want to hide! *Glancing at Elsie*: But I wasn't all that young! A man of thirty-two sees a guest changing out of a wet bathing suit in his bedroom . . .

Elsie, as he approaches, turns to him and her robe slips off one shoulder.

. . . and she stands there with her two bare faces hanging out.

ELSIE: Oh, are you through working? Why don't you swim now? The water's just right.

QUENTIN—*a laugh of great pain, crying out*: I tell you I didn't believe she knew she was naked!

Louise enters and sits at right, as though on the ground. Elsie descends to join her and Quentin follows her with his eyes.

It's Eden! . . . Well, because she was *married*! How could a woman who can tell when the Budapest String Quartet is playing off key; who refuses to wear silk stockings—*Lou enters upstage, reading a brief*—because the Japanese are invading Manchuria; whose husband, my friend, a saintly professor of law, is editing my first appeal to the Supreme Court on the grass outside that window—I could see the top of his head past her tit, for God's sake! Of course I saw, but it's what you allow yourself to admit! To admit what you see endangers principles!

Quentin turns to Louise and Elsie seated on the ground. They are talking in an intense whisper. He now approaches them from behind. Halts, turns to the Listener.

And you know? When two women are whispering, and they stop abruptly when you appear . . .

ELSIE AND LOUISE, *turning to him after an abrupt stop to their talking*: Hi.

QUENTIN: The subject must have been sex. And if one of them is your wife . . . she must have been talking about you. ·

ELSIE, *as though to get him to go*: Lou's behind the house, reading your brief. He says it's superb!

QUENTIN: I hope so, Elsie. I've been kind of nervous about what he'd say.

ELSIE: I wish you'd tell him that, Quentin! Will you? Just how much his opinion means to you. It's important you tell him. It's so enchanting here. *Taking in Louise, standing*: I envy you both so much!

> She goes upstage, pausing beside her husband, Lou. He is *a very tender, kindly man in shorts; he is absorbed in reading the brief.*

I want one more walk along the beach before the train. Did you comb your hair today?

LOU: I think so. *Closing the brief, coming down to Quentin*: Quentin! This is superb! It's hardly like a brief at all; there's a majestic quality, like a classic opinion! *Elsie exits. Lou, chuckling, tugs Quentin's sleeve*. I almost feel honored to have known you!

QUENTIN: I'm so glad, Lou—

LOU, *with an arm around Louise*: Your whole career will change with this! Could I ask a favor?

QUENTIN: Oh, anything, Lou.

LOU: Would you offer it to Elsie, to read? I know it seems an extraordinary request, but—

QUENTIN: No, I'd be delighted.

LOU: It's shaken her terribly—my being subpoenaed and all those damned headlines. Despite everything, it does affect one's whole relationship. So any gesture of respect—for example I gave her the manuscript of my new textbook and I've even called off publication for a while to incorporate her criticisms. It may be her psychoanalysis, but she's become remarkably acute—

LOUISE: My roast! *She exits upstage.*

QUENTIN: But I hope you don't delay it too long, Lou; it'd be wonderful to publish something now. Just to show those bastards.

LOU, *glancing behind him*: But you see, it's a textbook for the schools, and Elsie feels that it will only start a new attack on me.

QUENTIN: But they've investigated you. What more damage could they do?

LOU: Another attack might knock me off the faculty. It's only Mickey's vote that saved me the last time. He made a marvelous speech at the dean's meeting when I refused to testify.

QUENTIN: Well, that's Mickey.

LOU: Yes, but Elsie feels—I'd just be drawing down the lightning again to publish now. And yet to put that book away is like a kind of suicide to me—everything I know is in that book.

QUENTIN: Lou, you have a right to publish; a radical past is not leprosy—we only turned left because it seemed the truth was there. You mustn't be ashamed.

LOU, *in pain*: Goddammit, yes! Except—I never told you this, Quentin. . . . *He holds his position, de-animated.*

QUENTIN, *to Listener, as he comes down to the edge of the stage*: Yes, the day the world ended and nobody was innocent again. God, how swiftly it all fell down!

LOU, *speaking straight front*: When I returned from Russia and published my study of Soviet law—I left out many things I saw. I lied. For a good cause, I thought, but all that lasts is the lie.

> *Elsie and Louise enter, talking together intimately and unheard.*

And it's so strange to me now—I have many failings, but I have never been a liar. And I lied for the Party, over and over, year after year. And that's why now, with this book of mine, I want so much to be true to myself! You see, it's no attack I fear, but being forced to defend my own incredible lies! *He turns, surprised, to see Elsie.*

ELSIE: Lou, I'm quite surprised. I thought we'd settled this.

Father and Dan appear upstage.

LOU: Yes, dear, I only wanted Quentin's feeling—

ELSIE: Your shirt's out, dear.

He quickly tucks it into his shorts. And she turns to Quentin.

You certainly don't think he ought to publish.

QUENTIN: But the alternative seems—

ELSIE, *with a volcanic, suppressed alarm*: But, dear, that's the *situation!* Lou's not like you, Quentin; you and Mickey can function in the rough-and-tumble of private practice, but Lou's a purely academic person. He's *incapable* of going out and—

Upstage, Mother appears beside Father.

LOU, *with a difficult grin and chuckle*: Well, dear, I'm not all that delicate, I—

ELSIE, *with a sudden flash of contempt, to Lou*: This is hardly the time for illusions!

MOTHER: You *idiot!*

Quentin is shocked, turns quickly to Mother, who stands accusingly over the seated Father.

My *bonds?*

QUENTIN, *watching Mother go*: Why do I think of things falling apart? Were they ever whole?

Mother exits; for a moment Father and Dan stay on in darkness, frozen in their despair.

Louise now stands up.

LOUISE: Quentin?

He turns his eyes to the ground, then to the Listener. . . .

QUENTIN: Wasn't that a terrifying thing, what Holga said?

LOUISE: I've decided to go into psychoanalysis.

QUENTIN: To take up your life—like an idiot child?

LOUISE: I want to talk about some things with you.

QUENTIN: But can anybody really do that? Kiss his life?

LOUISE, *at a loss for an instant*: Sit down, will you?

She gathers her thoughts. He hesitates, as though pained at the memory, and also because at the time he lived this it was an agony. And as he approaches his chair . . .

QUENTIN, *to the Listener*: It was like—a meeting. In seven years we had never had a meeting. Never, never what you'd call—a meeting.

LOUISE: We don't seem—*A long pause while she peers at a forming thought*—married.

QUENTIN: We?

It is sincere, what she says, but she has had to learn the words, so there is the faintest air of a formula in her way of speaking.

LOUISE: You don't pay any attention to me.

QUENTIN, *to help her*: You mean like Friday night? When I didn't open the car door for you?

LOUISE: Yes, that's part of what I mean.

QUENTIN: But I told you; you always opened the car door for yourself.

LOUISE: I've always done everything for myself, but that doesn't mean it's right. Everybody notices it, Quentin.

QUENTIN: What?

LOUISE: The way you behave toward me. I don't exist. People are supposed to find out about each other. I am not all this uninteresting. Many people, men *and* women, think I *am* interesting.

QUENTIN: Well, I—*He breaks off.* I—don't know what you mean.

LOUISE: You have no conception of what a woman is.

QUENTIN: But I do pay attention—just last night I read you my whole brief.

LOUISE: Quentin, you think reading a brief to a woman is talking to her?

QUENTIN: But that's what's on my mind.

LOUISE: But if that's all on your mind, what do you need a wife for?

QUENTIN: Now what kind of a question is that?

LOUISE: Quentin, that's the question!

QUENTIN, *after a slight pause, with fear, astonishment*: What's the question?

LOUISE: What am I to you? Do you—do you ever *ask* me anything? Anything personal?

QUENTIN, *with rising alarm*: But Louise, what am I supposed to ask you? I *know* you!

LOUISE: No. *She stands with dangerous dignity.* You don't know me. *Pause. She proceeds now with caution.* I don't intend to be ashamed of myself any more. I used to think it was normal, or even that you don't see me because I'm not worth seeing. But I think now that you don't really see any woman. Except in some ways your mother. You do sense her feelings; you do know when she's unhappy or anxious, but not me. Or any other woman.

Elsie appears on second platform, about to drop her robe as before.

QUENTIN: That's not true, though. I—

LOUISE: Elsie's noticed it too.

QUENTIN, *guiltily snapping away from the vision of Elsie*: What?

LOUISE: She's amazed at you.

QUENTIN: Why, what'd she say?

LOUISE: She says you don't seem to notice when a woman is *present*.

QUENTIN: Oh. *He is disarmed, confused, and silent.*

LOUISE: And you know how she admires you. *Elsie disappears. Quentin nods seriously. Suddenly he turns to the Listener and bursts into an agonized, ironical laughter. He abruptly breaks it off and returns to silence before Louise. With uncertainty; it is her first attempt at confrontation*: Quentin?

He stands in silence.

Quentin?

He is silent.

Silence is not going to solve it any more, Quentin. I can't live this way.

Pause. Quentin gathers courage.

QUENTIN: Maybe I don't speak because the one time I did tell you my feelings you didn't get over it for six months.

LOUISE, *angered*: It wasn't six months, it was a few weeks. I did overreact, but it's understandable. You come back from a trip and tell me you'd met a woman you wanted to sleep with.

QUENTIN: That's not the way I said it.

LOUISE: It's exactly the way. And we were married a year.

QUENTIN: It is not the way I said it, Louise. It was an idiotic thing to tell you, but I still say I meant it as a compliment; that I did not touch her because I realized what you meant to me. And for damn near a year you looked at me as though I were some kind of a monster who could never be trusted again. *Immediately to the Listener*: And why do I believe she's right! That's the point! Yes—now, now! It's innocence, isn't it? The innocent are always better, aren't they? Then why can't I be innocent?

The tower appears.

Even this slaughterhouse! Why does something in me bow its head like an accomplice in this place!

Mother appears upstage.

Huh? Please, yes, if you think you know. *Turning to Mother*: In what sense treacherous?

MOTHER: What poetry he brought me! He understood me, Strauss. And two weeks after the wedding, Papa hands me the menu. To *read!*

QUENTIN: Huh! Yes! And to a little boy—who knows how to read; a powerful reader, that little boy!

MOTHER: I want your handwriting beautiful, darling; I want you to be . . .

QUENTIN, *realizing*: . . . an accomplice!

MOTHER, *turning on Father, who still sits dejectedly*: My *bonds?* And you don't even tell me anything. Are you a moron? You idiot!

QUENTIN, *watching her and Father go dark, to the Listener*: But why is the world so treacherous?

· 30 ·

Mickey appears upstage, faces Louise in silence.

Shall we lay it all to mothers? Aren't there mothers who keep dissatisfaction hidden to the grave, and do not split the faith of sons until they go in guilt for what they did not do? And I'll go further—here's the final bafflement for me—is it altogether good to be not guilty for what another does?

Father and Dan exit in darkness. The tower goes dark.

MICKEY, *to Louise, grinning*: You proud of him?

LOUISE: Yes!

MICKEY, *coming to Quentin, who turns to him*: The brief is fine, kid; it almost began to move me.

LOUISE: Lou and Elsie are here.

MICKEY: Oh! I didn't know. You look wonderful, Louise. You look all excited.

LOUISE: Thanks! It's nice to hear! *She shyly, soundlessly laughs, glancing at Quentin, and goes.*

MICKEY: You got trouble?

QUENTIN, *embarrassed*: I don't think so, she's going into psycho-analysis.

MICKEY: You got trouble. *Shakes his head, laughing thoughtfully.* I think maybe you got married too young; I did too. Although, *you* don't fool around, do you?

QUENTIN: I don't, no.

MICKEY: Then what the hell are you so guilty about?

QUENTIN: I didn't know I was till lately.

MICKEY: You know, when it first happened to me, I set aside five minutes a day just imagining my wife as a stranger. As though I hadn't made her yet. You got to generate some respect for her mystery. Start with five minutes; I can go as long as an hour, now.

QUENTIN: Makes it seem like a game, though, doesn't it?

MICKEY: Well, it is, isn't it, in a way? As soon as there's two people, you can't be absolutely sincere, can you? I mean she's not your rib.

QUENTIN: I guess that's right, yes.

Pause. Lou and Elsie are heard offstage. Mickey walks to a point, looks down as over a cliff.

MICKEY: Dear Lou; look at him down there, he never learned how to swim, always paddled like a dog. *Comes back.* I used to love that man. I still do. Quentin, I've been subpoenaed.

QUENTIN, *shocked*: Oh, God! The Committee?

MICKEY: Yes. I wish you'd have come into town when I called you. But it doesn't matter now.

QUENTIN: I had a feeling it was something like that. I guess I— I didn't want to know any more. I'm sorry, Mick. *To Listener*: Yes, not to see! To be innocent!

A long pause. They find it hard to look directly at each other.

MICKEY: I've been going through hell, Quent. It's strange—to have to examine what you stand for; not theoretically, but on a life-and-death basis. A lot of things don't stand up.

QUENTIN: I guess the main thing is not to be afraid.

MICKEY, *after a pause*: I don't think I am now.

A pause. Both sit staring ahead. Finally Mickey turns and looks at Quentin, who now faces him. Mickey tries to smile.

You may not be my friend any more.

QUENTIN, *trying to laugh it away—a terror rising in him*: Why?

MICKEY: I'm going to tell the truth.

Pause.

QUENTIN: How do you mean?

MICKEY: I'm—going to name names.

QUENTIN, *incredulously*: Why?

MICKEY: Because—I want to. Fifteen years, wherever I go, whatever I talk about, the feeling is always there that I'm deceiving people.

QUENTIN: But why couldn't you just tell about yourself?

Maggie enters, lies down on second platform.

MICKEY: They want the names, and they mean to destroy anyone who—

QUENTIN: I think it's a mistake, Mick. All this is going to pass, and I think you'll regret it. And anyway, Max has always talked against this kind of thing!

MICKEY: I've had it out with Max. I testify or I'll be voted out of the firm.

QUENTIN: I can't believe it! What about DeVries?

MICKEY: DeVries was there, and Burton, and most of the others. I wish you'd have seen their faces when I told them. Men I've worked with for thirteen years. Played tennis; intimate friends, you know? And as soon as I said, "I had been"—stones.

The tower lights.

QUENTIN, *to the Listener*: Everything is one thing! You see— I don't know what we are to one another!

MICKEY: I only know one thing, Quent, I want to live a straightforward, open life!

Lou enters in bathing trunks, instantly overjoyed at seeing Mickey. The tower goes dark.

Lou: Mick! I *thought* I heard your voice! *Grabs his hand.* How are you!

> *Lou and Mickey de-animate in an embrace. Holga appears with flowers on upper level.*

Quentin, *glancing up at Holga*: How do you dare make promises again? I have lived through all the promises, you see?

> *Holga exits.*

Lou, *resuming, moving downstage with Mickey*: Just the question of publishing my book, now. Elsie's afraid it will wake up all the sleeping dogs again.

Mickey: But don't you have to take that chance? I think a man's got to take the rap, Lou, for what he's done, for what he is. After all, it's your work.

Lou: I feel exactly that way! *Grabs his arm, including Quentin in his feeling.* Golly, Mick! Why don't we get together as we used to! I miss all that wonderful talk! Of course I know how busy you are now, but—

Mickey: Elsie coming up?

Lou: You want to see her? I could call down to the beach. *He starts off, but Mickey stops him.*

Mickey: Lou.

Lou, *sensing something odd*: Yes, Mick.

Quentin, *facing the sky*: Dear God.

Mickey: I've been subpoenaed.

Lou: No! *Mickey nods, looks at the ground. Lou grips his arm.* Oh, I'm terribly sorry, Mick. But can I say something—it might ease your mind; once you're in front of them it all gets remarkably simple!

Quentin: Oh dear God!

LOU: Everything kind of falls away excepting—one's self. One's truth.

MICKEY, *after a slight pause*: I've already been in front of them, Lou. Two weeks ago.

LOU: Oh! Then what do they want with you again?

MICKEY, *after a pause, with a fixed smile on his face*: I asked to be heard again.

LOU, *puzzled, open-eyed*: Why?

MICKEY—*he carefully forms his thought*: Because I want to tell the truth.

LOU, *with the first rising of incredulous fear*: In—what sense? What do you mean?

MICKEY: Lou, when I left the hearing room I didn't feel I had spoken. Something else had spoken, something automatic and inhuman. I asked myself, what am I protecting by refusing to answer? Lou, you must let me finish! You must. The Party? But I despise the Party, and have for many years. Just like you. Yet there is something, something that closes my throat when I think of telling names. What am I defending? It's a dream now, a dream of solidarity. But the fact is, I have no solidarity with the people I could name—excepting for you. And not because we were Communists together, but because we were young together. Because we—when we talked it was like some brotherhood opposed to all the world's injustice. Therefore, in the name of that love, I ought to be true to myself now. And the truth, Lou, my truth, is that I think the Party *is* a conspiracy—let me finish. I think we *were* swindled; they took our lust for the right and used it for Russian purposes. And I don't think we can go on turning our backs on the truth simply because reactionaries are saying it. What I propose—is that we try to separate our love for one another from this political morass. And I've said nothing just now that we haven't told each other for the past five years.

LOU: Then—what's your proposal?

MICKEY: That we go back together. Come with me. And answer the questions.

LOU: Name—the names?

MICKEY: Yes. I've talked to all the others in the unit. They've agreed, excepting for Ward and Harry. They cursed me out, but I expected that.

LOU, *dazed*: Let me understand—you are asking my permission to name me?

Pause.

You may not mention my name. *He begins physically shaking.* And if you do it, Mickey, you are selling me for your own prosperity. If you use my name I will be dismissed. You will ruin me. You will destroy my career.

MICKEY: Lou, I think I have a right to know exactly why you—

LOU: Because if everyone broke faith there would be no civilization! That is why that Committee is the face of the Philistine! And it astounds me that you can speak of truth and justice in relation to that gang of cheap publicity hounds! Not one syllable will they get from me! Not one word from my lips! No—your eleven-room apartment, your automobile, your money are not worth this.

MICKEY, *stiffened*: That's a lie! You can't reduce it all to money, Lou! *That* is false!

LOU, *turning on him*: There is only one truth here. You are terrified! They have bought your soul!

Elsie appears upstage, listening. Louise enters, watches.

MICKEY, *angrily, but contained*: And yours? Lou! Is it all yours, your soul?

Lou, *beginning to show tears*: How dare you speak of my—

Mickey, *quaking with anger*: You've got to take it if you're going to dish it out, don't you? Have you really earned this high moral tone—this perfect integrity? I happen to remember when you came back from your trip to Russia; and I remember who made you throw your first version into my fireplace!

Lou, *with a glance toward Elsie*: The idea!

Mickey: I saw you burn a true book and write another that told lies! Because she demanded it, because she terrified you, because she has taken your soul!

Lou, *shaking his fist in the air*: I condemn you!

Mickey: But from your conscience or from hers? Who is speaking to me, Lou?

Lou: You are a monster!

> Lou *bursts into tears, walks off toward Elsie; he meets her in the near distance; her face shows horror. At the front of stage Mickey turns and looks across the full width toward Quentin at the farthest edge of light, and . . .*

Mickey, *reading Quentin's feelings*: I guess you'll want to get somebody else to go over your brief with you. *Pause.* Quent—

> *Quentin, indecisive, but not contradicting him, now turns to him.*

Good-by, Quentin.

Quentin, *in a dead tone*: Good-by, Mickey.

> *Mickey goes out.*

Elsie: He's a *moral* idiot!

> *Holga enters above. Quentin turns to Elsie; something perhaps in his gaze or in the recesses of her mind makes her close her robe, which she holds tightly shut.*

Isn't that *incredible?*

> *Louise exits.*

QUENTIN, *quietly*: Yes.

ELSIE: After such friendship! Such love`between them! And for so many years!

> *She goes to Lou. Lifts him and tenderly leads him off.*

> *The camp tower comes alive, and Quentin moves out of this group, slowly toward it, looking up.*

> *Holga descends, carrying flowers. She is a distance away from Quentin, who turns to her.*

QUENTIN: You—love me, don't you?

HOLGA: Yes.

> *An instant's hesitation, and he turns quickly to Listener and cries out.*

QUENTIN: Is it that I'm looking for some simple-minded constancy that never is and never was?

> *Holga exits. Now Louise approaches him. They are alone.*

LOUISE: Quentin, I'm trying to understand why you got so angry with me at the party the other night.

QUENTIN: I wasn't *angry;* I simply felt that every time I began to talk you cut in to explain what I was about to say. *He goes and gets a sheaf of paper, sits.*

LOUISE: Well, I'd had a drink; I was a little high; I felt happy, I guess, that you weren't running for cover when everybody else was.

QUENTIN: Yes, but Max was there and DeVries, and they don't feel they're running for cover. I only want to win Lou's case, not some moral victory over the firm—I felt you were putting me out on a limb.

LOUISE: Quentin, I saw you getting angry when I was talking about that new anti-virus vaccine.

He tries to remember, believing she is right.

What is it? The moment I begin to assert myself it seems to threaten you. I don't think you *want* me to be happy.

QUENTIN—*there is a basic concession made by his tone of admitted bewilderment*: I tell you the truth, Louise, I don't think I feel very sure of myself any more. I'm glad I took on Lou, but it only hit me lately that no respectable lawyer would touch him. It's like some unseen web of connection between people is simply not there. And I always relied on it, somehow; I never quite believed that people could be so easily disposed of. And it's larger than the political question. I think it's got me a little scared.

LOUISE, *with a wish for his sympathy, not accusing*: Well, then, you must know how I felt when I found that letter in your suit.

QUENTIN, *turning to her, aware*: I didn't do that to dispose of you, Louise. *She does not reply.* I thought we'd settled about that girl. Is that what this is about? *She still does not reply.* You mean you think I'm still—

LOUISE, *directly at him*: I don't know what you're doing. I thought you told the truth about that other girl years ago, but after what happened again this spring—I don't know anything.

QUENTIN, *after a pause*: Tell me something; until this party the other night—in fact this whole year, I thought you seemed much happier. I swear to God, Louise, I thought we were building something till the other night!

LOUISE: But why?

QUENTIN: I've been trying like hell to show what I think of you. You've seen that, haven't you?

LOUISE: Quentin, you are full of resentment against me, you think I'm blind?

QUENTIN: What I resent is being forever on trial, Louise. Are you an innocent bystander here?

LOUISE: I said I did contribute; I demanded nothing for much too long.

QUENTIN: You mean the summer before last you didn't come to me and say that if I didn't change you would divorce me?

LOUISE: I never said I was *planning* a—

QUENTIN: You said if it came down to it you would divorce me—that's not a contribution?

LOUISE: Well, it certainly ought not send a man out to play doctor with the first girl he could lay his hands on.

QUENTIN: How much shame do you want me to feel? I hate what I did. But, I think I've explained it—I felt like nothing; I shouldn't have, but I did, and I took the only means I knew to—

LOUISE: This is exactly what I mean Quentin—you are still defending it. Right now.

He is stopped by this truth.

QUENTIN: Look, you're—not at all to blame, hey?

LOUISE: But how?

QUENTIN: Well, for example—you never turn your back on me in bed?

LOUISE: I never turned my—

QUENTIN: You have turned your back on me in bed, Louise, I am not insane!

LOUISE: Well, what do you expect? Silent, cold, you lay your hand on me?

QUENTIN, *fallen*: Well, I—I'm not very demonstrative, I guess. *Slight pause. He throws himself on her compassion.* Louise—I worry about you all day. And all night.

· 40 ·

LOUISE—*it is something, but not enough*: Well, you've got a child; I'm sure that worries you.

QUENTIN, *deeply hurt*: Is that all?

LOUISE, *with intense reasonableness*: Look, Quentin, you want a woman to provide an—atmosphere, in which there are never any issues, and you'll fly around in a constant bath of praise—

QUENTIN: Well, I wouldn't mind a little praise, what's wrong with praise?

LOUISE: Quentin, I am not a praise machine! I am not a blur and I am not your mother! I am a separate person!

QUENTIN, *staring at her, and what lies beyond her*: I see that now.

LOUISE: It's no crime! Not if you're adult and grown-up!

QUENTIN, *quietly*: I guess not. But it bewilders me. In fact, I got the same idea when I realized that Lou had gone from one of his former students to another and none would take him—

LOUISE: What's Lou got to do with it? I think it's admirable that you—

QUENTIN: Yes, but I am doing what you call an admirable thing because I can't bear to be—a separate person. I think so. I really don't want to be known as a Red lawyer; and I really don't want the newspapers to eat me alive; and if it came down to it Lou could defend himself. But when that decent, broken man who never wanted anything but the good of the world sits across my desk—I don't know how to say that my interests are no longer the same as his, and that if he doesn't change I consign him to hell because we are separate persons!

LOUISE: You are completely confused! Lou's case has nothing—

QUENTIN, *grasping for his thought*: I am telling you my confusion! I think Mickey also became a separate person—

LOUISE: You're incredible!

QUENTIN: I think of my mother, I think she almost became—

LOUISE: Are you identifying *me* with—

QUENTIN: Louise, I am asking you to explain this to me because this is when I go blind! When you've finally become a separate person, what the hell is there?

LOUISE, *with a certain unsteady pride*: Maturity.

QUENTIN: I don't know what that means.

LOUISE: It means that you know another person exists, Quentin. I'm not in analysis for nothing.

QUENTIN, *questing*: It's probably the symptom of a typical case of some kind, but I swear, Louise, if you would just once, of your own will, as right as you are—if you would come to me and say that something, something important was your fault and that you were sorry, it would help.

> *In her pride she is silent, in her refusal to be brought down again.*

Louise?

LOUISE: Good God! What an idiot! *She exits.*

QUENTIN: Louise . . .

> *He looks at his papers, the lights change. A sprightly music is heard. Anonymous park loungers appear and sit or lie about.*

How few the days are that hold the mind in place; like a tapestry hung on four or five hooks. Especially the day you stop becoming; the day you merely are. I suppose it's when the principles dissolve, and instead of the general gray of what ought to be you begin to see what is. Even the bench by the park seems alive, having held so many actual men. The word "now" is like a bomb through the window, and it ticks.

An old woman crosses with a caged parrot.

Now a woman takes a parrot for a walk. What will happen to it when she's gone? Everything suddenly has consequences.

A plain girl in tweeds passes, reading a paperback.

And how bravely a homely woman has to be! How disciplined of her, not to set fire to the Museum of Art.

A Negro appears, in pantomime asking for a light, which Quentin gives him.

And how does he keep so neat, and the bathroom on another floor? He must be furious when he shaves.

The Negro hurries off, seeing his girl.

Alone: And whatever made me think that at the end of the day I absolutely had to go home?

Maggie appears, looking about for someone, as Quentin sits on "park bench."

Now there's a truth; symmetrical, lovely skin, undeniable.

MAGGIE: 'Scuse me, did you see a man with a big dog?

QUENTIN: No. But I saw a woman with a little bird.

MAGGIE: No, that's not him. Is this the bus stop?

QUENTIN: Ya, the sign says—

MAGGIE, *sitting beside him:* I was standing over there and a man came with this big dog and just put the leash in my hand and walked away. So I started to go after him but the dog wouldn't move. And then this other man came and took the leash and went away. But I don't think it's really his dog. I think it's the first man's dog.

QUENTIN: But he obviously doesn't want it.

MAGGIE: But maybe he wanted for me to have it. I think the other man just saw it happening and figured he could get a free dog.

QUENTIN: Well, you want the dog?

MAGGIE: How could I keep a dog? I don't even think they allow dogs where I live. What bus is this?

QUENTIN: Fifth Avenue. This is the downtown side. Where do you want to go?

MAGGIE, *after thinking*: Well, I could go there.

QUENTIN: Where?

MAGGIE: Downtown.

QUENTIN: Lot of funny things go on, don't they?

MAGGIE: Well, he probably figured I would like a dog. Whereas I would if I had a way to keep it, but I don't even have a refrigerator.

QUENTIN: Yes. That must be it. I guess he thought you had a refrigerator.

She shrugs. Pause. He looks at her as she watches for the bus. He has no more to say.

LOUISE, *appearing*: You don't talk to any woman—not like a *woman*! You think reading your brief is *talking* to me?

She exits. In tension Quentin leans forward, arms resting on his knees. He looks at Maggie again.

QUENTIN, *with an effort*: What do you do?

MAGGIE, *as though he should know*: On the switchboard. *Laughs.* Don't you remember me?

QUENTIN, *surprised*: Me?

MAGGIE: I always sort of nod to you every morning through the window.

QUENTIN, *after an instant*: Oh. In the reception room!

MAGGIE: Sure! Maggie! *Points to herself.*

QUENTIN: Of course! You get my numbers sometimes.

MAGGIE: Did you think I just came up and started talking to you?

QUENTIN: I had no idea.

MAGGIE—*laughs*: Well, what must you have thought! I guess it's that you never saw me altogether. I mean just my head through that little window.

QUENTIN: Well, it's nice to meet all of you, finally.

MAGGIE—*laughs*: You go back to work again tonight?

QUENTIN: No, I'm just resting for a few minutes.

MAGGIE, *with a sense of his loneliness*: Oh. That's nice to do that. *She looks idly about. He glances down her body as she rises.* Is that my bus down there?

QUENTIN: I'm not really sure where you want to go. . . .

A man appears, eyes her, glances up toward the bus, back to her, staring.

MAGGIE: I wanted to find one of those discount stores; I just bought a phonograph but I only have one record. I'll see you! *She is half backing off toward the man.*

MAN: There's one on Twenty-seventh and Sixth Avenue.

MAGGIE, *turning, surprised*: Oh, thanks!

QUENTIN, *standing*: There's a record store around the corner, you know.

MAGGIE: But is it discount?

QUENTIN: Well, they all discount—

MAN, *slipping his hand under her arm*: What, ten per cent? Come on, honey, I'll get you an easy fifty per cent off.

MAGGIE, *to the man, starting to move off with him*: Really? But a Perry Sullivan . . . ?

MAN: Look, I'll give it to you—I'll give you two Perry Sullivans. Come on!

MAGGIE—*she halts, suddenly aware, disengages her arm, backs*: 'Scuse me, I—I—forgot something.

MAN, *reaching toward her*: Look, I'll give you ten records. *Calls off*: Hold that door! *Grabs her*. Come on!

QUENTIN, *moving toward him*: Hey!

MAN, *letting her go, to Quentin*: Ah, get lost! *He rushes off*. Hold it, hold the door!

Quentin watches the "bus" go by, then turns to her. She is absorbed in arranging her hair—but with a strangely doughy expression, removed.

QUENTIN: I'm sorry, I thought you knew him.

MAGGIE: No. I never saw him.

QUENTIN: Well—what were you going with him for?

MAGGIE: He said he knew a store. Where's the one you're talking about?

QUENTIN: I'll have to think a minute. Let's see . . .

MAGGIE: Could I sit with you? While you're thinking?

QUENTIN: Sure!

They return to the bench. He waits till she is seated; she is aware of the politeness, glances at him as he sits. Then she looks at him fully, for some reason amazed.

· 46 ·

That happen to you very often?

MAGGIE, *factually*: Pretty often.

QUENTIN: It's because you talk to them.

MAGGIE: But they talk to me, so I have to answer.

QUENTIN: Not if they're rude. Just turn your back.

MAGGIE—*she thinks about that, and indecisively*: Oh, okay. *As though remotely aware of another world, his world*: Thanks, though—for stopping it.

QUENTIN: Well, anybody would.

MAGGIE: No, they laugh. I'm a joke to them. You—going to rest here very long?

QUENTIN: Just a few minutes. I'm on my way home—I never did this before.

MAGGIE: Oh! You look like you always did. Like you could sit for hours under these trees, just thinking.

QUENTIN: No. I usually go right home. *Grinning*: I've always gone right home.

MAGGIE: See, I'm still paying for the phonograph, whereas they don't sell records on time, you know.

QUENTIN: They're afraid they'll wear out, I guess.

MAGGIE: Oh, that must be it! I always wondered. 'Cause you *can* get phonographs. How'd you know that?

QUENTIN: I'm just guessing.

MAGGIE, *laughing*: I can never guess those things! I don't know why they do anything half the time! *She laughs more deeply. He does.* I had about ten or twenty records in Washington, but my friend got sick, and I had to leave. *Pause. Thinks.* His family lived right over there on Park Avenue.

QUENTIN: Oh. Is he better?

MAGGIE: He died. *Tears come into her eyes quite suddenly.*

QUENTIN, *entirely perplexed*: When was this?

MAGGIE: Friday. Remember they closed the office for the day?

QUENTIN: You mean—*Astounded*—Judge Cruse?

MAGGIE: Ya.

QUENTIN: Oh, I didn't know that you—

MAGGIE: Yeah.

QUENTIN: He was a great lawyer. And a great judge too.

MAGGIE, *rubbing tears away*: He was very nice to me.

QUENTIN: I was at the funeral; I didn't see you, though.

MAGGIE, *with difficulty against her tears*: His wife wouldn't let me come. I got into the hospital before he died. But the family pushed me out and—I could hear him calling, "Maggie . . . Maggie!" *Pause.* They kept trying to offer me a thousand dollars. But I didn't want anything, I just wanted to say good-by to him! *She opens her purse, takes out an office envelope, opens it.* I have a little of the dirt. See? That's from his grave. His chauffeur drove me out—Alexander.

QUENTIN: Did you love him very much?

MAGGIE: No. In fact, a couple of times I really left him.

QUENTIN: Why didn't you altogether?

MAGGIE: He didn't want me to.

QUENTIN: Oh. *Pause.* So what are you going to do now?

MAGGIE: I'd love to get that record if I knew where they had a discount—

QUENTIN: No, I mean in general.

MAGGIE: Why, they going to fire me now?

QUENTIN: Oh, I wouldn't know about that.

MAGGIE: Although I'm not worried. Whereas I can always go back to hair.

QUENTIN: To where?

MAGGIE: I used to demonstrate hair preparations. *Laughs, squirts her hair with an imaginary bottle.* You know, in department stores? I was almost on TV once. *Tilting her head under his chin*: It's because I have very thick hair, you see? I have my mother's hair. And it's not broken. You notice I have no broken hair? Most women's hair is broken. Here, feel it, feel how—*She has lifted his hand to her head and suddenly lets go of it.* Oh, 'scuse me!

QUENTIN: That's all right!

MAGGIE: I just thought you might want to feel it.

QUENTIN: Sure.

MAGGIE: Go ahead. I mean if you want to. *She leans her head to him again. He touches the top of her head.*

QUENTIN: It is, ya! Very soft.

MAGGIE, *proudly*: I once went from page boy to bouffant in less than ten minutes!

QUENTIN: What made you quit?

A student sitting nearby looks at her.

MAGGIE: They start sending me to conventions and all. You're supposed to entertain, you see.

QUENTIN: Oh yes.

MAGGIE: There were parts of it I didn't like—any more. *She looks at the student, who turns away in embarrassment.* Aren't they sweet when they look up from their books!

The student walks off, mortified. She turns with a laugh to Quentin. He looks at her warmly, smiling. A clock strikes eight in a distant tower.

QUENTIN: Well, I've got to go now.

MAGGIE: 'Scuse me I put your hand on my head.

QUENTIN: Oh, that's all right. I'm not *that* bad. *He laughs softly, embarrassed.*

MAGGIE: It's not bad to be shy.

Pause. They look at each other.

QUENTIN: You're very beautiful, Maggie.

She smiles, straightens as though his words had entered her.

And I wish you knew how to take care of yourself.

MAGGIE: Oh . . . *Holding a ripped seam in her dress*: I got this torn on the bus this morning. I'm going to sew it home.

QUENTIN: I don't mean that.

She meets his eyes again—she looks chastised.

Not that I'm criticizing you. I'm not at all. You understand?

She nods, absorbed in his face.

MAGGIE: I understand. I think I'll take a walk in the park.

QUENTIN: You shouldn't. It's getting dark.

MAGGIE: But it's beautiful at night. I slept there one night when it was hot in my room.

QUENTIN: God, you don't want to do that. *Glancing at the park loungers*: Most of the animals around here are not in the zoo.

MAGGIE: Okay. I'll get a record, then. 'Scuse me about my hair if I embarrassed you.

QUENTIN, *laughing*: You didn't.

MAGGIE, *touching the top of her head as she backs away*: It's just that it's not broken. *He nods.* I'm going to sew this home. *He nods. She indicates the park, upstage.* I didn't *mean* to sleep there. I just fell asleep.

Several young men now rise, watching her.

QUENTIN: I understand.

MAGGIE: Well . . . see you! *Laughs.* If they don't fire me!

QUENTIN: 'By.

She passes two men who walk step for step behind her, whispering in her ear together. She doesn't turn or answer. Now a group of men is beginning to surround her. Quentin, in anguish, goes and draws her away from them.

Maggie! *He takes a bill from his pocket, moving her across stage.* Here, why don't you take a cab? It's on me. Go ahead, there's one right there! *Points and whistles upstage and right.* Go on, grab it!

MAGGIE: Where—where will I tell him to go but?

QUENTIN: Just cruise in the Forties—you've got enough there.

MAGGIE: Okay, 'by! *Backing out*: You—you just going to rest more?

QUENTIN: I don't know.

MAGGIE: Golly, that's nice!

The men walk off as Louise enters between Quentin and Maggie, continuing to her seat downstage. Maggie turns and goes to the second platform and lies down as before. Quentin moves down toward Louise, stands a few yards from her, staring at her optimistically. She remains unaware of him, reading.

QUENTIN: Yes. She has legs, breasts, mouth, eyes . . . how beautiful! A woman of my own! What a miracle! In my own house! *He bends and kisses Louise who looks up at him surprised, perplexed, lighting a cigarette.* Hi. *She keeps looking up at him, aware of some sea-like opening in the world.* What's the matter? *She still doesn't speak.* Well, what's the matter?

LOUISE: Nothing.

> *She returns to her book. Mystified, disappointed, he stands watching, then opens his briefcase and begins taking out papers.*

Close the door if you're going to type.

QUENTIN: I always do.

LOUISE: Not always.

QUENTIN: Almost always. *He almost laughs, he feels loose, but she won't be amused, and returns again to her book.* How about eating out tomorrow night? Before the parents' meeting?

LOUISE: What parents' meeting?

QUENTIN: The school.

LOUISE: That was tonight.

QUENTIN, *shocked*: Really?

LOUISE: Of course. I just got back.

QUENTIN: Why didn't you remind me when I called today? You know I often forget those things. I told you I wanted to talk to her teacher.

LOUISE, *just a little more sharply*: People do what they want to do, Quentin. *An unwilling shout:* And you said you had to work tonight! *She returns to her book.*

QUENTIN: I didn't work.

LOUISE, *keeping to her book*: I know you didn't work.

QUENTIN, *surprised, an alarm beginning*: How did you know?

LOUISE: Well, for one thing, Max called here at seven-thirty.

QUENTIN: Max? What for?

LOUISE: Apparently the whole executive committee was in his office, waiting to meet with you tonight. *His hand goes to his head; open alarm shows on his face.* He called three times, as a matter of fact.

QUENTIN: My God, I— How could I do that? What's his home number?

LOUISE: The book is in the bedroom.

QUENTIN: We were supposed to discuss my handling Lou's case. DeVries stayed in town tonight just to—settle everything. *Breaks off.* What's Max's number, Murray Hill 3 . . . what is it?

LOUISE: The book is next to the bed.

QUENTIN: You remember it, Murray Hill 3, something.

LOUISE: It's in the book.

Pause. He looks at her, puzzled.

I'm not the keeper of your phone numbers. You can remember them just as well as I. Please don't use that phone, you'll wake' her up.

QUENTIN, *turning*: I had no intention of calling in there.

LOUISE: I thought you might want to be private.

QUENTIN: There's nothing "private" about this. This concerns the food in your mouth. The meeting was called to decide whether I should separate from the firm until Lou's case is over—or permanently, for all I know. *Remembering the number, he goes to the phone.* I've got it—Murray Hill 3 . . .

She watches him go to the phone. He picks it up, dials one digit. And much against her will . . .

LOUISE: That's the old number.

QUENTIN: Murray Hill 3-4598.

LOUISE: It's been changed. *A moment.* Cortland 7-7098.

QUENTIN—*she is not facing him; he senses what he thinks is victory*: Thanks. *Starts again to dial, puts down the phone.* I don't know what to say to him. *She is silent.* We arranged for everybody to come back after dinner. It'll sound idiotic that I forgot about it.

LOUISE: You were probably frightened.

QUENTIN: But I made notes all afternoon about what I would say tonight! It's incredible!

LOUISE, *with an over-meaning*: You probably don't realize how frightened you are.

QUENTIN: I guess I don't. He said a dreadful thing today—Max. He was trying to argue me into dropping Lou and I said, "We should be careful not to adopt some new behavior just because there's hysteria in the country." I thought it was a perfectly ordinary thing to say but he—he's never looked at me that way, like we were suddenly standing on two distant mountains; and he said, "I don't know of any hysteria. Not in this office."

LOUISE: But why does all that surprise you? Max is not going to endanger his whole firm to defend a Communist. You tend to make relatives out of people.

QUENTIN: You mean . . .

LOUISE: I mean you can't have everything; if you feel this strongly about Lou you probably will have to resign.

QUENTIN, *after a pause*: You think I should?

LOUISE: That depends on how deeply you feel about Lou.

QUENTIN: I'm trying to determine that; I don't know for sure. What do you think?

LOUISE, *in anguish*: It's not my decision, Quentin.

QUENTIN, *puzzled and surprised*: But aren't you involved?

LOUISE: Of course I'm involved.

QUENTIN: I'm only curious how you—

LOUISE: You? Curious about me?

QUENTIN: Oh. We're not talking about what we're talking about, are we?

LOUISE, *nodding in emphasis*: You have to decide what you feel about a certain human being. For once in your life. And then maybe you'll decide what you feel about other human beings. Clearly and decisively.

QUENTIN: In other words . . . where was I tonight.

LOUISE: I don't care where you were tonight.

QUENTIN, *after a pause*: I sat by the park for a while. And this is what I thought. *With difficulty*: I don't sleep with other women, but I think I behave as though I do. *She is listening; he sees it and is enlivened by hope*. Maybe I invite your suspicion in order to—to come down off some bench, to stop judging others so perfectly. Because I do judge, and harshly too, when the fact is I'm bewildered. I wonder if I left that letter for you to read about that girl—in order somehow to start being real. *Against his own trepidation but encouraged by her evident uncertainty*: I met a girl tonight. Just happened to come by, one of the phone operators in the office. I probably shouldn't tell you this, but I will. Quite stupid, silly kid. Sleeps in the park, her dress ripped. She said some ridiculous things. But one thing struck me; she wasn't defending anything, upholding anything, or accusing—she was just *there*, like a tree or a cat. And I felt strangely abstract beside her. And I saw that we are killing one another with abstractions. I'm defending Lou because I love him, yet the society transforms that love into a kind of treason, what they call an issue, and I end up suspect and hated. Why can't we speak with the voice that speaks below the "issues"—with our real uncertainty? I came home just now—and I had a tremendous wish to come out—to you. And you to me. It sounds absurd, but this city is full of people rushing to meet one another. This city is full of lovers.

LOUISE: And what did she say?

QUENTIN: I guess I shouldn't have told you about it.

LOUISE: Why not?

QUENTIN: Louise, I don't know what's permissible to say any more.

LOUISE, *nodding*: You don't know how much to hide.

QUENTIN, *angering*: All right, let's not hide anything; it would have been easy to make love to her. *Louise reddens, stiffens.* And I didn't because I thought of you, and in a new way—like a stranger I had never gotten to know. And by some miracle you were waiting for me, in my own home.

LOUISE: What do you want, my congratulations? You don't imagine a real woman goes to bed with any man who happens to come along? Or that a real man goes to bed with every woman who'll have him? Especially a slut, which she obviously is?

QUENTIN: How do you know she's a—

LOUISE, *laughing*: Oh, excuse me, I didn't mean to insult her! You're unbelievable! Suppose I came home and told you I'd met a man on the street I wanted to go to bed with—because he made the city seem full of lovers.

QUENTIN, *humiliated*: I understand. I'm sorry. I would get angry too but I would see that you were struggling. And I would ask myself—maybe I'd even be brave enough to ask you—how *I* had failed.

LOUISE: Well, you've given me notice; I get the message. *She starts out.*

QUENTIN: Louise, don't you ever doubt yourself? Is it enough to prove a case, to even win it—*Shouts*—when we are dying?

Mickey enters at the edge of the stage. Elsie enters on second platform, opening her robe as before.

LOUISE, *turning, in full possession*: I'm not dying. I'm not the one who wanted to break this up. And that's all it's about. It's all it's been about the last three years. You don't want me. *She goes out.*

QUENTIN, *to himself*: God! Can that be true?

MICKEY: There's only one thing I can tell you for sure, kid—don't ever be guilty.

QUENTIN: Yes! *Seeking strength, he stretches upward.* Yes! *But his conviction wavers; he turns toward the vision.* But if you had felt more guilt, maybe you wouldn't have . . .

ELSIE, *closing her robe*: He's a moral idiot!

QUENTIN: Yes! That is right. And yet . . . What the hell is moral? And what am I, to even ask that question? A man ought to know—a decent man knows that like he knows his own face!

Louise enters with a folded sheet and a pillow.

LOUISE: I don't want to sleep with you.

QUENTIN: Louise, for God's sake!

LOUISE: You are disgusting!

QUENTIN: But in the morning Betty will see . . .

LOUISE: You should have thought of that.

The phone rings. He looks at sheets, makes no move to answer.

Did you give her this number?

It rings again.

Did you give her this number? *With which she strides to the phone.* Hello! Oh, yes. He's here. Hold on, please.

QUENTIN: I can't sleep out here; I don't want her to see it. *He goes to the phone with a look of hatred.*

LOUISE: It's Max.

Surprised, he takes the phone from her.

QUENTIN, *into phone*: Max? I'm sorry, the whole thing just slipped my mind. I don't know how to explain it, I just went blank, I guess. *Pause.* The radio? No, why? . . . *What?* When? *Long pause.* Thanks . . . for letting me know. Yes, he was. Good night . . . Ya, see you in the morning. *Hangs up. Pause. He stands staring.*

LOUISE: What is it?

QUENTIN: Lou. Was killed by a subway train tonight.

LOUISE—*gasps*: How?

QUENTIN: They don't know. They say "fell or jumped."

LOUISE: He couldn't have! The crowd must have pushed him!

QUENTIN: There is no crowd at eight o'clock. It was eight o'clock.

LOUISE: But *why?* Lou *knew* himself! He knew where he *stood!* It's impossible!

QUENTIN, *staring*: Maybe it's not enough—to know yourself. Or maybe it's too much. I think he did it.

LOUISE: But *why?* It's inconceivable!

QUENTIN: When I saw him last week he said a dreadful thing. I tried not to hear it. *Pause. She waits.* That I turned out to be the only friend he had.

LOUISE, *genuinely*: Why is that dreadful?

QUENTIN, *evasively, almost slyly*: It just was. I don't know why. *Tears forming in his eyes, he comes toward Listener.* I didn't

· 58 ·

dare know why! But I dare now. It was dreadful because I was not his friend either, and he knew it. I'd have stuck it to the end but I hated the danger in it for myself, and he saw through my faithfulness; and he was not telling me what a friend I was, he was praying I would be—"Please be my friend, Quentin" is what he was saying to me, "I am drowning, throw me a rope!" Because I wanted out, to be a good American again, kosher again—and proved it in the joy . . . the joy . . . the joy I felt now that my danger had spilled out on the subway track! So it is not bizarre to me.

The tower blazes into life, and he walks with his eyes upon it.

This is not some crazy aberration of human nature to me. I can easily see the perfectly normal contractors and their cigars, the carpenters, plumbers, sitting at their ease over lunch pails; I can see them laying the pipes to run the blood out of this mansion; good fathers, devoted sons, grateful that someone else will die, not they, and how can one understand that, if one is innocent? If somewhere in one's soul there is no accomplice—of that joy, that joy, that joy when a burden dies . . . and leaves you safe?

Maggie's difficult breathing is heard. He turns in pain from it, comes to a halt on one side of the sheets and pillow lying on the floor at Louise's feet.

I've got to sleep; I'm very tired. *He bends to pick up the sheets. She makes an aborted move to pick up the pillow.*

LOUISE, *with great difficulty*: I—I've always been proud you took Lou's case. *He picks up sheets and pillow, stands waiting.* It was —courageous. *She stands there, empty-handed, not fully looking at him.*

QUENTIN: I'm glad you feel that way. *But he makes no move either. The seconds are ticking by. Neither can let down his demand for apology, or grace. With difficulty*: And that you told me. Thanks.

LOUISE: But—you are honest, that way. I've often told you.

QUENTIN: Recently?

LOUISE: Good night.

She starts away, and he feels the unwillingness with which she leaves.

QUENTIN: Louise, if there's one thing I've been trying to do it's to be honest with you.

LOUISE: No, you've been trying to keep the home fires burning and see the world at the same time.

QUENTIN: So that all I am is deceptive and cunning.

LOUISE: Not all, but mostly.

QUENTIN: And there is no struggle. There is no pain. There is no struggle to find a way back to you?

LOUISE: That isn't the struggle.

QUENTIN: Then what are you doing here?

LOUISE: I—

QUENTIN: What the hell are you compromising yourself for if you're so goddamned honest!

He starts a clench-fisted move toward her and she backs away, terrified and strangely alive. Her look takes note of the aborted violence, and she is very straight and yet ready to flee.

LOUISE: I've been waiting for the struggle to begin.

He is dumbstruck—by her sincerity, her adamance. With a straight look at him, she turns and goes out.

QUENTIN, *alone, and to himself*: Good God, can there be more? Can there be worse? *Turning to the Listener*: See, that's what's incredible to me—three years more! What did I expect to save us? Suddenly, God knows why, she'd hold out her hand and I hold out mine, and laugh, laugh it all away, laugh it all back to—her dear, honest face looking up to mine . . . *Breaks off, staring into the distance. Far upstage, Louise looks at him with pride, as of old.* Back to some everlasting smile that saves. That's maybe why I came; I think I still believe it. That underneath we're all profoundly friends! I can't believe this world; all this hatred isn't real to me! *Turns back to his "living room," the sheets. Louise is gone now.* To bed down like a dog in my living room, how can that be necessary? Then go in to her, open your heart, confess the lechery, the mystery of women, say it all. . . . *He has moved toward where she exited, now halts.* But I did that. So the truth, after all, may merely be murderous? The truth killed Lou, destroyed Mickey. Then how do you live? A workable lie? But that comes from a clear conscience! Or a dead one. Not to see one's own evil—there's power! And rightness too!—so kill conscience. Kill it. *Glancing toward her exit:* Know all. admit nothing, shave closely, remember birthdays, open car doors, pursue Louise not with truth but with attention. Be uncertain on your own time, in bed be absolute. And thus be a man—and join the world. And in the morning, a dagger in that dear little daughter's heart! *Flinging it toward Louise's exit:* Bitch! *Sits.* I'll say I have a cold. Didn't want to give it to Mommy. *With disgust:* Pah! Papapapapa. *Sniffs, tries to talk through his nose.* Got a cold in my nose, baby girl . . .

He groans. Pause. He stares; stalemate. A jet plane is heard. An airport porter appears, carrying two bags, as Holga, dressed for travel, moves onto the highest level, looking about for Quentin. A distant jet roars in take-off. Quentin glances at his watch, and, coming down to the chair . . .

Six o'clock, Idlewild. *Now he glances up at Holga, who is still looking about her as in a crowd.* It's that the evidence is bad for promises. But how else do you touch the world—except with a promise? And yet, I must not forget the way I wake; I open up my eyes each morning like a boy, even now; even now. That's as true as anything I know, but where's the evidence? Or is it simply that my heart still beats? . . . Certainly, go ahead, I'll wait.

He follows the departing Listener with his eyes; now he rises, follows "him" upstage.

You don't mind my staying? I'd like to settle this. Although actually, I—*Laughs*—only came to say hello.

He turns front. He stares ahead; a different kind of relaxation is on him now, alone. The stage is dark but for a light on him. Now the tower is seen, and Maggie on the second platform near him. Suddenly she raises herself up.

MAGGIE: Quentin? Quentin?

QUENTIN, *in agony*: I'll get to it, honey. *He closes his eyes.* I'll get to it.

He strikes sparks from a lighter held to a cigarette. All light is gone.

Act Two

The stage is dark. A spark is seen, a flame fires up. When the stage illuminates, Quentin is discovered lighting his cigarette—no time has passed. He continues to await the Listener's return and walks a few steps in thought, and as he does a jet plane is heard, and the airport announcer's voice: ". . . from Frankfurt is now unloading at gate nine, passengers will please . . ." It becomes a watery garble, and at the same moment Holga, as before, walks onto the upper level with the airport porter, who leaves her bags and goes. She looks about as in a crowd, then, seeing "Quentin," stands on tiptoe and waves.

HOLGA: Quentin! Here! Here! *She opens her arms as he evidently approaches.* Hello! Hello!

He turns from her to the returned Listener at front and comes to him downstage. Holga moves out.

QUENTIN: Oh, that's all right, I didn't mind waiting. How much time do I have?

He sits at the forward edge of the stage, looks at his watch. Maggie appears on the second platform, in a lace wedding dress; Lucas, a designer, is on his knees, finishing the vast hem. Carrie, a Negro maid, stands by, holding her veil. Maggie is nervous, on the edge of life, looking into a mirror.

I think I can be clearer now.

MAGGIE, *in an ecstasy of fear and hope*: All right, Carrie, tell him to come in! *As though trying the angular words*: My *husband*!

CARRIE, *walking a few steps to a point, where she halts*: You can see her now, Mr. Quentin.

They are gone. Quentin continues to the Listener.

QUENTIN: I am bewildered by the death of love. And my responsibility for it.

Holga moves into light again, looking about for him at the airport.

This woman's on my side; I have no doubt of it. And I wouldn't want to outlive another accusation. Not hers.

Holga exits. He stands, agitated.

I suddenly wonder why I risk it again. Except . . .

Felice and Mother appear.

You ever felt you once saw yourself—absolutely true? I may have dreamed it, but I swear that somewhere along the line—with Maggie, I think—for one split second I saw my life; what I had done, what had been done to me, and even when I ought to do. And that vision sometimes hangs behind my head, blind now, bleached out like the moon in the morning; and if I could only let in some necessary darkness it would shine again. I think it had to do with power.

Felice approaches, about to remove the bandage.

Maybe that's why she sticks in my mind. *He walks around her, peering*. Well, that's power, isn't it? To influence a girl to change her nose, her life? . . . It does, yes, it frightens me, and I wish to God—*Felice raises her arm*—she'd stop blessing me! *Mother exits on upper platform. He laughs uneasily, surprised at the force of his fear*. Well, I suppose because there is a fraud involved; I have no such power.

Maggie suddenly appears in man's pajamas, talking into a phone, coming down to the bed, center.

MAGGIE, *with timid idolatry*: Hello? Is— How'd you know it's me? *Laughs as she lies down.* You really remember me? Maggie? From that park that day? Well, 'cause it's almost four years so I . . .

He comes away from her as she continues talking, unheard.

QUENTIN, *to the Listener, glancing from Maggie to Felice*: I do, yes, I see the similarity.

Laughter is heard as Holga appears at a café table, an empty chair beside her, the music of a café fiddle in the air.

HOLGA, *to an empty seat beside her*: I love the way you eat! You eat like a Pasha, a grand duke!

QUENTIN, *to Listener, looking toward her*: Yes, adored again! But . . . there is something different here. *As he moves toward Holga, he says to Listener*: Now keep me to my theme, I spoke of power.

He sits beside her. As he speaks now, Holga's aspect changes; she becomes moody, doesn't face him, seems hurt. And, sitting beside her, he speaks to the Listener.

We were in a café one afternoon in Salzburg, and quite suddenly, I don't know why—it all seemed to be dying between us. And I saw it all happening again. You know that moment, when you begin desperately to talk about architecture?

HOLGA: Fifteen thirty-five. The Archbishop designed it himself.

QUENTIN: Beautiful.

HOLGA, *distantly*: Yes.

QUENTIN, *as though drawing on his courage, suddenly turning to her*: Holga. I thought I noticed your pillow was wet this morning.

· 65 ·

HOLGA: It really isn't anything important.

QUENTIN: There are no unimportant tears.

HOLGA: I feel sometimes—*Breaks off, then*: —that I'm boring you.

LOUISE, *entering upstage*: I am not all this uninteresting, Quentin!

He stares at her, trying to join this with his lost vision, and in that mood he turns out to the Listener.

QUENTIN: The question is power, but I've lost the . . . Yes! *He springs up and circles Louise.* I tell you there were times when she looked into the mirror and I saw she didn't like her face, and I wanted to step between her and her suffering.

HOLGA: I may not be all that interesting.

QUENTIN, *of Louise*: I felt guilty even for her face! But . . . with her—*He returns to the café table*—there was some new permission . . . not to blind her to her own unhappiness. I saw that it belonged to her as mine belonged to me. And suddenly there was only good will and a mystery.

HOLGA: I wish you'd believe me, Quentin; you have no duty here.

QUENTIN: Holga, I would go. But I know I'd be looking for you tomorrow.

Mother enters, taking Holga's place on the seat beside him. He continues speaking without pause.

But there's truth in what you feel. The time does come when I feel I must go. Not toward anything, or away from you. . . . But there *is* some freedom in the going.

MOTHER: Darling, there is never a depression for great people! The first time I felt you move, I was standing on the beach at Rockaway. . . .

Quentin has gotten up.

QUENTIN, *to Listener*: But power. Where is the . . .

MOTHER: And I saw a star, and it got bright, and brighter, and brighter! And suddenly it fell, like some great man had died, and you were being pulled out of me to take his place, and be a light, a light in the world!

QUENTIN, *to Listener*: Why is there some . . . air of treachery in that?

FATHER, *suddenly appearing with Dan behind him, to Mother*: What the hell are you talking about? We're just getting started again. I need him!

Quentin avidly turns from one to the other as they argue.

MOTHER: You've got Dan, you don't need him! He wants to try to get a job, go to college maybe.

FATHER: He's got a job!

MOTHER: He means with pay! I don't want his young years going by. He wants a life!

FATHER, *indicating Dan; they have surrounded Quentin*: Why don't *he* "want a life"?

MOTHER: Because he's different!

FATHER: Because *he* knows what's right! *Indicating Mother and Quentin together*: You're two of a kind—what you "want"! Chrissake, when I was his age I was supporting six people! *He comes up to Quentin*. What are you, a stranger? What are you!

QUENTIN, *peering into the revulsion on his father's face*: Yes, I felt a power, in the going . . . and treason in it. Because there's failure, and you turn your back on failure . . .

Father exits with Mother.

FATHER: I need him!

DAN, *putting an arm around Quentin*: No, kid, don't feel that way. I just want to see him big again, but you go. I'll go back to school if things pick up.

QUENTIN, *peering at Dan, who has walked on past him and is talking to an invisible Quentin*: Yes, good men stay . . . although they die there . . .

DAN, *indicating a book in his hand, addressing an invisible Quentin*: It's my Byron, I'll put it in your valise, and I've put in my new Argyles, just don't wash them in hot water. And remember, kid, wherever you are . . . *A train whistle is heard far off. Dan rushes onto second platform, calling*: Wherever you are, this family's behind you! So buckle down, now, I'll send you a list of books to read.

Mother, Father, and Dan disappear, waving farewell. Felice is gone.

MAGGIE, *suddenly sitting up on her bed, addressing an empty space at the foot*: But could I read them?

QUENTIN, *spinning about in quick surprise*: Huh!

All the others have gone dark but him and Maggie.

MAGGIE: I mean what kind of books? 'Cause, see—I never really graduated high school. Although I always liked poetry.

QUENTIN—*breaks his stare at her and quickly comes down to the Listener*: It's that I can't find myself in this vanity any more.

MAGGIE, *enthralled, on bed*: I can't hardly believe you came! Can you stay five minutes? I'm a singer now, see? In fact—*With a laugh at herself*—I'm in the top three. And for a long time I been wanting to tell you that . . . none of it would have happened to me if I hadn't met you that day.

QUENTIN: Why do you speak of love? All I can see now is the power she offered me. All right. *Turns to her in conflict, and unwillingly.* I'll try. *He approaches her.*

MAGGIE: I'm sorry if I sounded frightened on the phone but I didn't think you'd be in the office after midnight. *Laughs at herself nervously.* See, I only pretended to call you. Can you stay like five minutes?

QUENTIN, *backing into the chair*: Sure. Don't rush.

MAGGIE: That's what I mean, you know I'm rushing! Would you like a drink? Or a steak? They have two freezers here. My agent went to Jamaica so I'm just staying here this week till I go to London Friday. It's the Palladium, like a big vaudeville house, and it's kind of an honor but I'm a little scared to go.

QUENTIN: Why? I've heard you; you're marvelous. Especially . . . *He can't remember a title.*

MAGGIE: No, I'm just flapping my wings yet. But did you read what that *News* fellow wrote? He keeps my records in the 'frigerator, case they melt!

QUENTIN—*laughs with her, then recalls*: "Little Girl Blue"! It's very moving, the way you do that.

MAGGIE: Really? 'Cause, see, it's not I say to myself, "I'm going to sound sexy," I just try to come *through*—like in love or . . . *Laughs.* I really can't believe you're here!

QUENTIN: Why? I'm glad you called; I've often thought about you the last couple of years. All the great things happening to you gave me a secret satisfaction for some reason.

MAGGIE: Maybe 'cause you did it.

QUENTIN: Why do you say that?

MAGGIE: I don't know, just the way you looked at me. I didn't even have the nerve to go see an agent before that day.

QUENTIN: *How did* I look at you?

MAGGIE, *squinching up her shoulders, a mystery*: Like . . . out of your *self*. Most people, they . . . just look *at* you. I can't explain it. And the way you talked to me . . .

LOUISE, *who has been sitting right, playing solitaire*: You think reading your brief is talking to me?

MAGGIE: What did you mean—it gave you a secret satisfaction?

QUENTIN: Just that—like in the office, I'd hear people laughing that Maggie had the world at her feet—

MAGGIE, *hurt, mystified*: They laughed!

QUENTIN: In a way.

MAGGIE, *in pain*: That's what I mean; I'm a joke to most people.

QUENTIN: No, it's that you say what you mean, Maggie. You don't seem to be upholding anything, you're not—ashamed of what you are.

MAGGIE: W—what do you mean, of what I am?

Louise looks up. She is playing solitaire.

QUENTIN, *suddenly aware he has touched a nerve*: Well . . . that you love life, and . . . It's hard to define, I . . .

LOUISE: The word is tart. But what did it matter as long as she praised you?

QUENTIN, *to Listener, standing, and moving within Maggie's area*: There's truth in it—I hadn't had a woman's praise, even a girl I'd laughed at with the others—

MAGGIE: But you didn't, did you?

He turns to her in agony.

Laugh at me?

QUENTIN: No. *He suddenly stands and cries out to Listener.* Fraud! From the first five minutes! . . . Because! I should have agreed she *was* a joke, a beautiful piece, trying to take herself seriously! Why did I lie to her, play this cheap benefactor, this—Listens, and now unwillingly he turns back to her.

MAGGIE: Like when you told me to fix where my dress was torn? You wanted me to be—proud of myself. Didn't you?

QUENTIN, *surprised*: I guess I did, yes. *To Listener*: By God I did!

MAGGIE, *feeling she has budged him*: Would you like a drink?

QUENTIN, *relaxing*: I wouldn't mind. *Glancing around*: What's all the flowers?

MAGGIE, *pouring*: Oh, that's that dopey prince or a king or whatever he is. He keeps sending me a contract—whereas I get a hundred thousand dollars if we ever divorce. I'd be like a queen or something, but I only met him in El Morocco *once! She laughs, handing him his drink.* I'm supposed to be his girl friend too! I don't know why they print those things.

QUENTIN: Well, I guess everybody wants to touch you now.

MAGGIE: Cheers! *They drink; she makes a face.* I hate the taste but I love the effect! Would you like to take off your shoes? I mean just to rest.

QUENTIN: I'm okay. I thought you sounded on the phone like something frightened you.

MAGGIE: Do you have to go home right away?

QUENTIN: Are you all alone here?

MAGGIE: It's okay. Oh hey! I cut your picture out of the paper last month. When you were defending that Reverend Harley Barnes in Washington? *Taking a small framed photo from under her pillow*: See? I framed it!

QUENTIN: Is something frightening you, Maggie?

MAGGIE: No, it's just you're here! It's odd how I found this—I went up to see my father—

QUENTIN: He must be very proud of you now.

MAGGIE, *laughing*: Oh, no—he left when I was eighteen months, see—'cause he said I wasn't from him, although my mother always said I was. And they keep interviewing me now and I never know what to answer, when they ask where you were born, and all. So I thought if he would just see me, and you know, just —look at me . . . I can't explain it.

QUENTIN: Maybe so you'll know who you are.

MAGGIE: Yes! But he wouldn't even talk to me on the phone—just said, "See my lawyer," and hung up. But on the train back there was your picture, right on the seat looking up at me. And I said, "I know who I am! I'm Quentin's friend!" But don't worry about it—I mean you could just be somebody's friend, couldn't you?

QUENTIN, *after a slight pause*: Yes, Maggie, I can be somebody's friend. It's just that you're so beautiful—and I don't only mean your body and your face.

MAGGIE: You wouldn't even have to see me again. I would do anything for you, Quentin—you're like a god!

QUENTIN: But anybody would have told you to mend your dress.

MAGGIE: No, they'd have laughed or tried for a quick one. You know.

QUENTIN, *to Listener*: Yes! It's all so clear—the honor! The first honor was that I hadn't tried to go to bed with her! She took it for a tribute to her "value," and I was only afraid! God, the hypocrisy! . . . But why do you speak of love?

MAGGIE: Oh hey! You know what I did because of you? *He turns back to her.* I was christening a submarine in the Groton shipyard; 'cause I was voted the favorite of all the workers! And I made them bring about ten workers up on the platform, whereas they're the ones built it, right? And you know what the admiral said? I better watch out or I'll be a Communist. And suddenly I thought of you and I said, "I don't know what's so terrible; they're for the poor people." Isn't that what you believe?

QUENTIN: I did, but it's a lot more complicated, honey.

MAGGIE: Oh! I wish I knew something.

QUENTIN: You know how to see it all with your own eyes, Maggie, that's more important than all the books.

MAGGIE: But you know if it's true. What you see.

QUENTIN, *puzzled*: You frightened *now*? . . . You are, aren't you? *Maggie stares at him in tension; a long moment passes.* What is it, dear? You afraid to be alone here? *Pause.* Why don't you call somebody to stay with you?

MAGGIE: I don't know anybody . . . like that.

QUENTIN, *after a slight pause*: Can I do anything? . . . Don't be afraid to ask me.

MAGGIE, *in a struggle, finally*: Would you . . . open that closet door?

QUENTIN—*looks off, then back to her*: Just open it?

MAGGIE: Yes.

He walks into the dark periphery; she sits up warily, watching. He opens a "door." He returns. And she lies back.

QUENTIN: Do you want to tell me something? I'm not going to laugh. *Sits.* What is it?

MAGGIE, *with great difficulty*: When I start to go to sleep before. And suddenly I saw smoke coming out of that closet under the door. Kept coming and coming. It start to fill the whole room!

She breaks off, near weeping. He reaches and takes her hand.

QUENTIN: Oh, kid—you've often dreamed such things, haven't you?

MAGGIE: But I was awake!

QUENTIN: Well it was a waking dream. It just couldn't stay down till you went to sleep. These things can be explained if you trace them back.

MAGGIE: I know. I go to an analyst.

QUENTIN: Then tell him about it, you'll figure it out.

MAGGIE: It's when I start to call you before. *She is now absorbed in her own connections.* See, my mother—she used to get dressed in the closet. She was very—like moral, you know? But sometimes she'd smoke in there. And she'd come out—you know? with a whole cloud of smoke around her.

QUENTIN: Well—possibly you felt she didn't want you to call me.

MAGGIE, *astounded*: How'd you know that?

QUENTIN: You said she was so moral. And here you're calling a married man.

MAGGIE: Yes! She tried to kill me once with a pillow on my face 'cause I would turn out bad because of—like her sin. And I have her hair, and the same back. *She turns half to him, showing a naked back.* 'Cause I have a good back, see? Every masseur says.

QUENTIN: Yes, it is. It's beautiful. But it's no sin to call me.

MAGGIE, *shaking her head like a child with a relieved laugh at herself*: Doesn't make me bad. Right?

QUENTIN: You're a very moral girl, Maggie.

MAGGIE, *delicately and afraid*: W—what's moral?

QUENTIN: You tell the truth, even against yourself. You're not pretending to be—*Turns out to the Listener, with a dread joy—* innocent! Yes, that suddenly there was someone who—could not club you to death with their innocence! And now it's all laughable!

Mother appears, raising her arm. Louise exits.

MOTHER: I saw a star . . .

MAGGIE: I bless you, Quentin! *Mother vanishes as he turns back to Maggie, who takes up his photo again.* Lots of nights, I take your picture, and I bless you. You mind? *She has pressed the picture against her cheek.*

QUENTIN: I hope you sleep.

MAGGIE: I will now! *Lies back.* Honestly! I feel . . . all clear!

QUENTIN, *with a wave of his hand*: Good luck in London.

MAGGIE: And—what's moral, again?

QUENTIN: To live the truth.

MAGGIE: That's you!

QUENTIN: Not yet, dear; but I intend to try. Don't be afraid to call me if you need any help. *She is suddenly gone. Alone, he continues the thought.* Any time—*Dan appears in crew-necked sweater with his book*—you need anything, you call, y'hear?

DAN: This family's behind you, Quentin. *Backing into darkness, with a wave of farewell as train whistle sounds*: Any time you need anything . . .

QUENTIN—*surprised, he has turned quickly to Dan, who disappears; and to the Listener, as he still stares at the empty space Dan has left*: You know? It isn't fraud, but some . . . disguise. I came to her like Dan—his goodness! No wonder I can't find myself!

> *Felice appears as Maggie exits. She is about to remove the bandage, and he grasps for the concept.*

And that girl the other night. When she left. It's still not clear, but suddenly those two fixtures on my wall. *He walks toward a "wall," looking up.* I didn't do it, but I wanted to. Like—*He turns and spreads his arms in crucifixion*—this! *In disgust, he lowers his arms.* I don't know! Because she . . . gave me something! The power to change her! As though I—*Cries out*—felt something for her! *He almost laughs.* What the hell am I trying to do, love *everybody*?

The line ends in self-contempt and anger. And suddenly, extremely fast, a woman appears in World War I costume —a Gibson Girl hat and veil over her face, ankle-length cloak, and in her hand a toy sailboat. She is bent over, as though offering the boat to a little boy, and her voice is like a whisper, distant, obscure. Father enters, calling, followed by Dan.

MOTHER: Quentin? Look what we brought you from Atlantic City—from the boardwalk!

The boy evidently runs away; Mother instantly is anxious and angering and rushes to a point and halts, as though calling through a closed door.

Don't lock this door! But darling, we didn't trick you, we took Dan because he's older and I wanted a rest! But Fanny told you we were coming back, didn't she? Why are you running that water? Quentin, stop that water! Ike, come quick! Break down the door! Break down the door! *She has rushed off into darkness.*

But a strange anger is on his face, and he has started after her. And to the Listener . . .

QUENTIN: They sent me out for a walk with the maid. When I came back the house was empty. God, why is betrayal the only truth that sticks? I adored that woman. It's monstrous I can't mourn her!

The park bench lights. Maggie appears in a heavy white man's sweater, a white angora skating cap over a red wig, moccasins and sun glasses.

MAGGIE, *to the empty bench*: Hi! It's me! Maggie!

QUENTIN: Or mourn her either. . . . No, it's not that I think I killed her. It's . . .

MAGGIE, *to the empty bench*: See? I told you nobody recognizes me!

QUENTIN: . . . that I can't find myself in it. Either the guilt comes or the innocence! But where's my love or even my crime? And I tell you I saw it once! I saw *Quentin* here!

MAGGIE: Golly, I fell asleep the minute you left, the other night! You like my wig? See? And moccasins!

Slight pause. Now he smiles, comes beside her on the bench.

QUENTIN: All you need is roller skates.

MAGGIE, *clapping her hands with joy*: You're funny!

QUENTIN, *half to Listener*: I keep forgetting—*Wholly to her*—how beautiful you are. Your eyes make me shiver.

She is silent for a moment, adoring.

MAGGIE: Like to see my new apartment? There's no elevator even, or a doorman. Nobody would know. If you want to rest before you go to Washington. *He doesn't reply.* 'Cause I just found out —I go to Paris after London.

QUENTIN: So . . . how long will you be gone?

MAGGIE: It's maybe two months, I think. *They both arrive at the same awareness—the separation is pain. Tears are in her eyes.* Quentin?

QUENTIN: Honey . . . *Takes her hand.* Don't look for anything more from me.

MAGGIE: I'm not! But if I went to Washington . . . I could register in the hotel as Miss None.

QUENTIN: N-u-n?

MAGGIE: No—"n-o-n-e"—like nothing. I made it up once 'cause I can never remember a fake name, so I just have to think of nothing and that's me! *She laughs with joy.* I've done it.

QUENTIN: It *is* a marvelous thought. The whole government's hating me, and meanwhile back at the hotel . . .

MAGGIE: That's what I mean! Just when that committee is knocking on your head you could think of me like naked—

QUENTIN: What a lovely thought!

MAGGIE: And it would make you happy.

QUENTIN, *smiling warmly at her*: And nervous.

MAGGIE: Because it should all be one one thing, you know? Helping people, and sex. You might even argue better the next day!

QUENTIN, *with a new awareness, astonishment*: You know? There's one word written on your forehead.

MAGGIE: What?

QUENTIN: "Now."

MAGGIE: But what else is there?

QUENTIN: A future. And I've been carrying it around all my life, like a vase that must never be dropped. So you can't ever touch anybody, you see?

MAGGIE: But why can't you just hold it in one hand?—*He laughs*—and touch with the other! I would never bother you, Quentin. *He looks at his watch, as though beginning to calculate if there might not be time. Maggie, encouraged, glances at his watch.* Just make it like when you're thirsty. And you drink and walk away, that's all.

QUENTIN: But what about you?

MAGGIE: Well . . . I would have what I gave.

QUENTIN: You're all love, aren't you?

MAGGIE: That's all I am! A person could die any minute, you

know. *Suddenly*: Oh, hey! I've got a will! *Digging into her pocket, she brings out a folded sheet of notepaper.* But is it legal if it's not typewritten?

QUENTIN, *taking it*: What do you want with a will? *He starts reading the will.*

MAGGIE: I'm supposed to be like a millionaire in about two years! And I've got to do a lot of flying now.

QUENTIN, *looking at her*: Who wrote this?

MAGGIE: Jerry Moon. He's a friend of my agent Andy in the building business, but he knows a lot about law. He signed it there for a witness. I saw him sign it. In my bedroom—

QUENTIN: It leaves everything to the agency.

MAGGIE: I know, but just for temporary, till I can think of somebody to put down.

QUENTIN: Don't you have anybody at all?

MAGGIE: No!

QUENTIN: What's all the rush?

MAGGIE: Well, in case Andy's plane goes down. He's got five children, see, and his—

QUENTIN: But do you feel responsible for his family?

MAGGIE: Well, no. But he did help me, he loaned me money when I—

QUENTIN: A million dollars?

Two boys enter upstage, carrying baseball gloves.

MAGGIE, *with a dawning awareness and fear*: Well, not a million . . .

QUENTIN: Who's your lawyer?

MAGGIE: Well, nobody.

QUENTIN, *with a certain unwillingness, even a repugnance about interfering—he sounds neutral*: Didn't anybody suggest you get your own lawyer?

MAGGIE: But if you trust somebody you trust them—don't you?

Slight pause. A decision seizes him; he takes her hand.

QUENTIN: Come on, I'll walk you home.

MAGGIE, *as she stands with him*: Okay! 'Cause what's good for Andy's good for me, right?

QUENTIN: I can't advise you, honey, maybe you get something out of this that I don't understand. Let's go.

MAGGIE: No! I'm not involved with Andy. I . . . don't really sleep around with everybody, Quentin! *He starts to take her but she continues.* I was with a lot of men but I never got anything for it. It was like charity, see. My analyst said I gave to those in need. Whereas, I'm not an institution. You believe me?

QUENTIN, *wanting her feverishly*: I believe you. Come on.

A small gang of boys with baseball equipment obstructs them; one of the first pair points at her.

BOY: It's Maggie, I told you!

MAGGIE, *pulling at Quentin's arm, defensively, but excited*: No, I just look like her, I'm Sarah None!

QUENTIN: Let's go! *He tries to draw her off, but the boys grab her, and she begins accepting pencils and pieces of paper to autograph.* Hey!

CROWD: How about an autograph, Maggie! Whyn't you come down to the club! When's your next spectacular! Hey, Mag, I got all your records! Sing something! *Handing over a paper for her to sign*: For my brother, Mag! Take off your sweater, Mag, it's hot out! How about that dance like you did on TV!—*A boy wiggles sensuously.*

QUENTIN: That's enough!

Quentin has been thrust aside; he now reaches in, grabs her, and draws her away as she walks backward, still signing, laughing with them. And into darkness, and the boys gone, and she turns to him.

MAGGIE: I'm sorry!

QUENTIN: It's like they're eating you. You like that?

MAGGIE: No, but they're just people. Could you sit down till the train? All I got so far is this French Provincial. *Taking off her sweater*: You like it? I picked it out myself. And my bed, and my record player. But it could be a nice apartment, couldn't it?

In silence Quentin takes her hand; now he draws her to him; now he kisses her.

MAGGIE: I love you, Quentin. I would do anything for you. And I would never bother you, I swear.

QUENTIN: You're so beautiful it's hard to look at you.

MAGGIE: You didn't even see me! *Backing away*: Why don't you just stand there and I'll come out naked! Or isn't there a later train?

QUENTIN, *after a pause*: Sure. There's always a later train. *He starts unbuttoning his jacket.*

MAGGIE: I'll put music!

QUENTIN—*now he laughs through his words*: Yeah, put music! *He strives for his moment; to the Listener as he opens his jacket:* Here; it was somewhere here! I don't know, a—a fraud!

A driving jazz comes on.

MAGGIE: Here, let me take off your shoes!

Father, Mother, Dan enter. Maggie drops to his feet, starting to unlace. Stiffly, with a growing horror, he looks down at her. Now shapes move in the darkness.

QUENTIN: Maggie?

MAGGIE, *looking up from the floor, leaving off unlacing*: Yes?

He looks around in the darkness; and suddenly his father charges forward.

FATHER: What you *want!* Always what you *want!* Chrissake, what are you!

Now Louise appears, reading a book, but Dan is standing beside her, almost touching her with his hand.

DAN: This family's behind you, kid.

And Mother, isolated, moving almost sensuously—and Quentin is pressed, as though by them, away from Maggie.

QUENTIN, *roaring out to all of them, his fists angrily in air against them*: But where is *Quentin?*

MOTHER: Oh, what poetry he brought me, Strauss, and novels to read . . .

QUENTIN, *going toward Mother in her longing*: Yes, yes! But I know that treason! And the terror of complicity in that desire; yes, and not to be unworthy of these loyal, failing men! But where is Quentin? Instead of taking off my clothes, this—posture! Maggie—

MAGGIE: Okay. Maybe when I get back . . .

QUENTIN: You . . . have to tear up that will. *To Listener*: Can't even go to bed without a principle! But how can you speak of love, she was chewed and spat out by a long line of grinning men! Her name floating in the stench of locker rooms and parlor-car cigar smoke! She had the truth that day, I brought the lie that she had to be "saved"! From what? Except my own contempt!

MAGGIE, *to the empty space where Quentin was*: But even my

analyst said it was okay. 'Cause a person like me has to have somebody.

QUENTIN: Maggie—honest men don't draw wills like that.

MAGGIE: But it's just for temporary—

QUENTIN: Darling, if I went to Andy, and this adviser, and the analyst too, perhaps—I think they'd offer me a piece, to shut up. They've got you on a table, honey, and they're carving you—

MAGGIE: But . . . I can't spend all that money anyway! I can't even *think* over twenty-five dollars!

QUENTIN: It's not the money they take, it's the dignity they destroy. You're not a piece of meat; you seem to think you owe people whatever they demand!

MAGGIE: I know. *She lowers her head with a cry, trembling with hope and shame.*

QUENTIN, *tilting up her face*: But Maggie, you're somebody! You're not a kid any more, running around looking for a place to sleep! It's not only your success or that you're rich—you're straight, you're serious, you're first-class, people *mean* something to you; you don't have to go begging shady people for advice like some—some tramp! *With a sob of love and desperation she slides to the floor and grasps his thighs, kissing his trousers. He watches, then suddenly lifts her, and with immense pity and hope*: Maggie, stand up!

> *The music flies in now, and she smiles strangely through her tears, and with a kind of statement of her persisting nature begins unbuttoning her blouse. Maggie's body writhes to the beat within her clothing. And as soon as she starts her dance, his head shakes—and to the Listener . . .*

No, not love; to stop impersonating, that's all! To live—Groping—to live in good faith if only with my guts! To—*To Dan and Father*: Yes! To be "good" no more! Disguised no more! *To Mother*: Afraid no more to show what Quentin, Quentin, Quentin—is!

LOUISE: You haven't even the decency to . . .

A high tribunal appears, and a flag; a chairman bangs his gavel once; he is flanked by others looking down on Quentin from on high.

QUENTIN: That decency is murderous! Speak truth, not decency. I curse the whole high administration of fake innocence! *To the chairman*: I declare it, I am not innocent!—nor good!

CHAIRMAN: But surely Reverend Barnes cannot object to answering whether he attended the Communist-run Peace Congress in Prague, Czechoslovakia. No—no, counsel will not be allowed to confer with the witness, this is not a trial! Any innocent man would be—

QUENTIN: And this question—innocent! How many Negroes you allow to vote in your patriotic district? And which of your social, political, or racial sentiments would Hitler have disapproved? And not a trial? You fraud, your "investigators" this moment are working in this man's church to hound him out of it!

HARLEY BARNES, *rising to his feet, wearing a clerical collar*: I decline on the grounds of the First and Fifth Amendments to the Constitution.

QUENTIN, *with intense sorrow*: But are we sure, Harley—I ask it, I ask it—if the tables were turned, and they were in front of you, would you permit *them* not to answer? Hateful men that they are? *Harley looks at him indignantly, suspiciously.* I am not sure what we are upholding any more—are we good by merely saying no to evil? Even in a righteous "no" there's some disguise. Isn't it necessary—to say—*Harley is gone, and the tribunal; Maggie is there, snapping her fingers, letting down her hair*—to finally say yes—to *something*? *Turning toward Maggie, who lies down on the bed*: Yes, yes, yes.

MAGGIE: Say anything to me.

QUENTIN, *looking down at her*: A fact . . . a fact . . . a fact, a thing.

MAGGIE: Sing inside me.

Quentin crosses to Listener.

QUENTIN: Even condemned, unspeakable like all truth!

MAGGIE: Become happy.

QUENTIN: Contemptible like all truth.

MAGGIE: That's all I am.

QUENTIN: Covered like truth with slime: blind, ignorant.

MAGGIE: But nobody ever said to me, stand up!

QUENTIN: The blood's fact, the world's blind gut—yes!

MAGGIE: Now.

QUENTIN, *sitting before the Listener, his back to Maggie*: To this, yes.

MAGGIE: Now . . . Now. *Pause.* Quentin? *She rises off the bed, drawing the blanket around her, and in a languid voice addresses a point upstage.* Quenny? That soap is odorless, so you don't have to worry. *Slight pause.* It's okay! Don't rush; I love to wait for you! *She glances down at the floor.* I love your shoes. You have good taste! *She moves upstage.* 'Scuse me I didn't have anything for you to eat, but I didn't know! I'll get eggs, though, case maybe in the mornings. And steaks—case at night. I mean just in case. You could have it just the way you want, just any time. *She turns, looking front.* Like me?

Holga appears above, in the airport, looking about for him.

QUENTIN, *to the Listener, his back to Maggie*: It's all true, but it isn't the truth. I know it because it all comes back so cheap; I loved that girl. My bitterness is making me lie. I'm afraid. To make a promise. *Glancing up at Holga*: Because I don't know who'll be making it. I'm a stranger to my life.

MAGGIE—*she has lifted a "tie" off the floor*: Oh, your tie got all wrinkled! I'm sorry! But hey, I have a tie! It's beautiful, a regular man's tie. *Catching herself*: I . . . just happen to have it! *She laughs it off and goes into darkness. Holga is gone.*

QUENTIN: I tell you, below this fog of tawdriness and vanity, there is a law in this disaster, and I saw it as hard and clear as a statute. But I think I saw it . . . with some love. Or can one ever remember love? It's like trying to summon up the smell of roses in a cellar. You might see a rose, but never the perfume. And that's the truth of roses, isn't it—the perfume?

> *On the second platform Maggie appears in light in a wedding dress; Carrie, a Negro maid, is just placing a veiled hat on her head; Lucas, a designer, is on his knees, hurriedly fixing the last hem, as before. Maggie is turning herself, wide-eyed, in an unseen mirror. Quentin begins to rise.*

MAGGIE: Hurry, Lucas, the ceremony is for three! Hurry, please! *Lucas sews faster.*

QUENTIN, *to Listener*: I want to see her with . . . that love again! Why is it so hard? Standing there, that wishing girl, that victory in lace.

MAGGIE, *looking ahead on the edge of life as Lucas bites off the last threads*: You won't hardly know me any more, Lucas! He saved me, I mean it! I've got a new will and I even changed my analyst—I've got a wonderful doctor now! And we're going to do all my contracts over, which I never got properly paid. And Ludwig Reiner's taking me! And he won't take even opera singers unless they're, you know, like artists! No matter how much you want to pay him. I didn't even dare, but Quentin made me go—and now he took me, Ludwig Reiner, imagine!

> *Now she turns, seeing Quentin entering. An awe of the moment takes them both; Lucas goes. Carrie lightly touches Maggie's forehead and silently prays.*

QUENTIN: Oh, my darling. How perfect you are.

MAGGIE, *descending toward him*: Like me?

Clergyman and woman guest enter on second platform.

QUENTIN: Good God! To come home every night—to *you!*

He starts for her, open-armed, laughing, but she touches his chest, excited and strangely fearful.

MAGGIE: You still don't have to do it, Quentin. I could just come to you whenever you want.

QUENTIN: You just can't believe in something good really happening. But it's real, darling, you're my wife!

MAGGIE, *with a hush of fear on her voice*: I want to tell you why I went into analysis.

QUENTIN: Darling, you're always making new revelations, but—

MAGGIE: But you said we have to love what happened, didn't you? Even the bad things?

QUENTIN, *seriously now, to match her intensity*: Yes, I did.

Clergyman and woman exit.

MAGGIE: I . . . was with two men . . . the same day.

She has turned her eyes from him. A group of wedding guests appears on second platform.

I mean the same day, see. *She almost weeps now, and looks at him, subservient and oddly chastened.* I'll always love you, Quentin. But we could just tell them we changed our mind—

QUENTIN: Sweetheart—an event itself is not important; it's what you took from it. Whatever happened to you, this is what you made of it, and I love this! *Quickly to Listener*: Yes!—that we conspired to violate the past, and the past is holy and its horrors are holiest of all! *Turning back to Maggie*: And . . . something . . . more . . .

MAGGIE, *with hope now*: Maybe . . . it would even make me a better wife, right?

QUENTIN: That's the way to talk!

Elsie enters above and joins group of guests.

MAGGIE, *with gladness, seeing a fruit of past pain*: 'Cause I'm not curious! You be surprised, these so-called respectable women, they smile and their husbands never know, but they're curious. But I *know* all that, so I know I have a king! But there's people who're going to laugh at you!

QUENTIN: Not any more, dear, they're going to see what I see. Come!

MAGGIE, *not moving with him*: What do you see? Tell me! *Bursting out of her*: 'Cause I think . . . you were ashamed once, weren't you?

QUENTIN: I see your suffering, Maggie; and once I saw it, all shame fell away.

MAGGIE: You . . . were ashamed!?

QUENTIN, *with difficulty*: Yes. But you're a victory, Maggie, you're like a flag to me, a kind of proof, somehow, that people can win.

Louise enters upstage, brushing her hair.

MAGGIE: And you—you won't ever look at any other woman, right?

QUENTIN: Darling, a wife can be loved!

MAGGIE, *with a new intensity of conflict*: Before, though—why did you kiss that Elsie?

QUENTIN: Just hello. She always throws her arms around people.

MAGGIE: But—why'd you let her rub her body against you?

QUENTIN, *laughing*: She wasn't rub—

MAGGIE, *downing a much greater anxiety*: I saw it. And you stood there.

QUENTIN, *trying to laugh*: Maggie, it was a meaningless gesture—

MAGGIE: You want me to be like I used to be—like it's all a fog? *Now pleadingly, and faintly wronged*: You told me yourself that I have to look for the meaning of things, didn't you? Why did you let her do that?

QUENTIN: She came up to me and threw her arms around me, what could I do?

MAGGIE, *in a flash of frightened anger*: Just tell her to knock it off!

QUENTIN, *taken aback*: I . . . don't think you want to sound like this, honey.

WOMAN GUEST: Ready! Ready!

> *The guests line up on the steps, forming a corridor for Maggie and Quentin.*

QUENTIN: Come, they're waiting.

> *He puts her arm in his; they turn to go. A wedding march is heard.*

MAGGIE, *almost in tears*: Teach me, Quentin! I don't know how to be! Forgive me I sounded that way.

QUENTIN, *as against the vision of Louise*: No. Say what you feel; the truth is on our side; always say it!

MAGGIE, *with a plea, but going on toward the guests*: You're not holding me!

QUENTIN, *half the stage away now, and turning toward the empty air, his arm still held as though he were walking beside her*: I am, darling, I'm with you!

MAGGIE, *moving along the corridor of guests*: I'm going to be a good wife. I'm going to be a good wife.

CARRIE: God bless this child.

MAGGIE, *faltering as she walks into darkness*: Quentin, I don't feel it!

The wedding march is gone. Louise exits upstage.

QUENTIN, *both frustrated and with an appeal to her, moving downstage with "her" on his arm*: I'm holding you! See everybody smiling, adoring you? Look at the orchestra guys making a V for victory! Everyone loves you, darling! Why are you sad?

Suddenly, from the far depths of the stage, she calls out with a laugh and hurries on in a fur coat, indicating a wall at front.

MAGGIE: Surprise! You like it? They rushed it while we were away!

QUENTIN—*they are half a stage apart*: Yes, it's beautiful!

MAGGIE: See how large it makes the living room? *Rushing toward left*: And I want to take down that wall too! Okay?

QUENTIN, *not facing in her direction; to his memory of it*: But we just finished putting those walls in.

MAGGIE: Well, it's only money; I want it big, like a castle for you!

QUENTIN: It's lovely, dear, but we're behind in the taxes.

MAGGIE: Used to say, I have one word written on my forehead. Why can't it be beautiful now? I get all that money next year.

QUENTIN: But you owe almost all of it—

MAGGIE: Don't hold the future like a vase—touch now, touch me! I'm here, and it's now!

She rushes into semi-darkness, where she is surrounded by Carrie, a dresser, and a secretary.

QUENTIN, *against himself, alone on the forestage*: Okay! Tear it

down! Make it beautiful! Do it now! Maybe I *am* too cautious . . .
Forgive me!

> *Her voice is suddenly heard in a recorded vocal number.
> He breaks into a genuine smile of joy and dances for a
> moment alone, as a group of executives surround Maggie.
> Now Maggie appears in a gold dress out of the group of
> cautiously listening executives. Quentin rushes to her.*

QUENTIN: Maggie, sweetheart—that's magnificent!

MAGGIE, *worried, uncertain*: No! Tell me the truth! That piano's
off, you're not listening!

> *A pianist, wearing sunglasses and smoking, emerges from the
> group listening to the record.*

QUENTIN: But nobody'll ever notice that!

MAGGIE: I notice it. Don't you want me to be good? I *told*
Weinstein I wanted Johnny Block, but they give me this fag
and he holds back my beat!

> *The pianist walks away, silently insulted.*

QUENTIN: But you said he's one of the best.

MAGGIE: I said Johnny Block was best, but they wouldn't pay
his price. I make millions for them and I'm still some kind of a
joke.

QUENTIN: Maybe I ought to talk to Weinstein. . . . *He hurries to
a point upstage.*

MAGGIE, *calling after him*: No, don't get mixed up in my crummy
business, you've got an important case—

QUENTIN: Weinstein, get her Johnny Block! *Turning back to her
as a new version of the number comes on*: There now! Listen
now! *She flies into his arms. The executives leave, gesturing their
congratulations.* See? There's no reason to get upset.

MAGGIE: Oh, thank you, darling!

QUENTIN: Just tell me and I'll talk to these people any time you . . .

The music goes out.

MAGGIE: See? They respect you. Ask Ludwig Reiner, soon as you come in the studio my voice flies! Oh, I'm going to be a good wife, Quentin, I just get nervous sometimes that I'm . . . only bringing you my problems. But I want my stuff to be perfect, and all they care is if they can get rich on it. *She sits dejectedly.*

QUENTIN: Exactly, dear—so how can you look to them for your self-respect? Come, why don't we go for a walk? We never walk any more. *Sits on his heels beside her.*

MAGGIE: You love me?

QUENTIN: I adore you. I just wish you could find some joy in your life.

MAGGIE: Quentin, I'm a joke that brings in money.

QUENTIN: I think it's starting to change though—you've got a great band now, and Johnny Block, and the best sound crew—

MAGGIE: Only because I fought for it. You'd think somebody'd come to me and say: Look, Maggie, you made us all this money, now we want you to develop yourself, what can we do for you?

QUENTIN: Darling, they'd be selling frankfurters if there were more money in it; how can you look to them for love?

Pause. Her loneliness floods in on her.

MAGGIE: But where will I look?

QUENTIN, *thrown down*: Maggie, how can you say that?

MAGGIE—*she stands; there is an underlying fear in her now*: When I walked into the party you didn't even put your arms around me. I felt like one of those *wives* or something!

QUENTIN: Well, Donaldson was in the middle of sentence and I—

MAGGIE: So what? I walked into the room! I hire him, he doesn't hire me!

Louise appears upstage in dim light; she is cold-creaming her face.

QUENTIN: But he is directing your TV show, and I was being polite to him.

MAGGIE: You don't have to be ashamed of me, Quentin. I had a right to tell him to stop those faggy jokes at my rehearsal. Just because he's cultured? I'm the one the public pays for, not Donaldson! Ask Ludwig Reiner what my value is!

QUENTIN: I married you, Maggie. I don't need Ludwig's lecture on your value.

MAGGIE, *looking at him with strange, unfamiliar eyes*: Why—why you so cold?

QUENTIN: I'm not cold, I'm trying to explain what happened.

MAGGIE: Well, take me in your arms, don't explain. *He takes her in his arms, he kisses her.* Not like that. *Hold* me.

QUENTIN—*he tries to hold her tighter, then lets go*: Let's go for a walk, honey. Come on.

MAGGIE, *sinking*: What's the matter?

QUENTIN: Nothing.

MAGGIE: But Quentin—you should look at me, like I *existed* or something. Like you used to look—out of your *self*.

Maggie moves away into darkness, meets maid, and changes into negligee.

QUENTIN, *alone*: I adore you, Maggie; I'm sorry; it won't ever happen again. *Louise exits.* Never! You need more love than I thought. But I've got it, and I'll make you see it, and when you do you're going to astound the world!

A rose light floods the bed; Maggie emerges in a dressing gown.

MAGGIE, *indicating out front*: Surprise! You like it? See the material?

QUENTIN: Oh, that's lovely! How'd you think of that?

MAGGIE: All you gotta do is close them and the sun makes the bed all rose.

QUENTIN, *striving for joy, embracing her on the bed*: Yes, it's beautiful! You see? An argument doesn't mean disaster! Oh, Maggie, I never knew what love was!

MAGGIE, *kissing him*: Case during the day, like maybe you get the idea to come home and we make love again in daytime. *She ends sitting in a weakness; nostalgically.* Like last year, remember? In the winter afternoons? And once there was still snow on your hair. See, that's all I am, Quentin.

QUENTIN: I'll come home tomorrow afternoon.

MAGGIE, *half humorously*: Well, don't *plan* it.

He laughs, but she looks at him strangely again, her stare piercing. His laugh dies.

QUENTIN: What is it? I don't want to hide things any more, darling. Tell me, what's bothering you?

MAGGIE, *shaking her head, seeing*: I'm not a good wife. I take up so much of your work.

QUENTIN: No, dear. I only said that because you—*Striving to soften the incident*—you kind of implied that I didn't fight the network hard enough on that penalty, and I got it down to twenty thousand dollars. They had a right to a hundred when you didn't perform.

MAGGIE, *with rising indignation*: But can't I be sick? I was sick!

QUENTIN: I know, dear, but the doctor wouldn't sign the affidavit.

MAGGIE, *furious at him*: I had a pain in my side, for Christ's sake, I couldn't stand straight! You don't believe me, do you!

QUENTIN: Maggie, I'm only telling you the legal situation.

MAGGIE: Ask Ludwig what you should do! You should've gone in there roaring! 'Stead of a polite liberal and affidavits—I shouldn't have had to pay anything!

QUENTIN: Maggie, you have a great analyst, and Ludwig is a phenomenal teacher, and every stranger you meet has all the answers, but I'm putting in forty per cent of my time on your problems, not just some hot air.

MAGGIE: You're not putting forty per cent of--

QUENTIN: Maggie, I keep a log, I know what I spend my time on!

> *She looks at him, mortally wounded, goes upstage to a secretary, who enters with an invisible drink. Maid joins them with black dress, and Maggie changes.*

I'm sorry, darling, but when you talk like that I feel a little like a fool. Don't start drinking, please.

MAGGIE: Should never have gotten married; every man I ever knew they hate their wives. I think I should have a separate lawyer.

QUENTIN, *alone on forestage*: Darling, I'm happy to spend my time on you; my greatest pleasure is to know I've helped your work to grow!

MAGGIE, *as a group of executives surrounds her*: But the only reason I went to Ludwig was so I could make myself an artist you'd be proud of! You're the first one that believed in me!

QUENTIN: Then what are we arguing about? We want the same thing, you see? *Suddenly to Listener*: Yes, power! To transform somebody, to save!

MAGGIE, *emerging from the group, wearing reading glasses*: He's a very good lawyer; he deals for a lot of stars. He'll call you to give him my files.

QUENTIN, *after a slight pause; hurt*: Okay.

MAGGIE: It's nothing against you; but like that girl in the orchestra, that cellist—I mean Andy took too much but he'd have gone in there and got rid of her. I mean you don't laugh when a singer goes off key.

QUENTIN: But she said she coughed.

MAGGIE, *furiously*: She didn't cough, she laughed!

QUENTIN: Now, Maggie.

MAGGIE: I'm not finishing this tape if she's in that band tomorrow! I'm entitled to my conditions, Quentin—and I shouldn't have to plead with my husband for my rights. I want her out!

The executives are gone.

QUENTIN: I don't know what the pleading's about. I've fired three others in three different bands.

MAGGIE: Well, so what? You're my husband. You're supposed to do that. Aren't you?

QUENTIN: But I can't pretend to enjoy demanding people be fired—

MAGGIE: But if it was your daughter you'd get angry, wouldn't you? Instead of apologizing for her?

QUENTIN, *envisioning it*: I guess I would, yes. I'm sorry. I'll do it in the morning.

MAGGIE, *with desperate warmth, joining him, sitting center*: That's all I mean. If I want something you should ask yourself why, why does she want it, not why she shouldn't have it. . . . That's why I don't smile, I feel I'm fighting all the time to make you *see*. You're like a little boy, you don't see the knives people hide.

QUENTIN: Darling, life is not all that dangerous. You've got a husband now who loves you.

Pause. She seems to fear greatly.

MAGGIE: When your mother tells me I'm getting fat, I know where I am. And when you don't do anything about it.

QUENTIN: But what can I do?

MAGGIE: Slap her down, that's what you do!

Secretary enters with imaginary drink, which Maggie takes.

QUENTIN: But she says anything comes into her head, dear—

MAGGIE: She insulted me! She's jealous of me!

QUENTIN: Maggie, she adores you. She's proud of you.

MAGGIE, *a distance away now*: What are you trying to make me think, I'm crazy? *Quentin approaches her, groping for reassurance.* I'm not crazy!

QUENTIN, *carefully*: The thought never entered my mind, darling. I'll . . . talk to her.

MAGGIE: Look, I don't want to see her any more. If she ever comes into this house, I'm walking out!

QUENTIN: Well, I'll tell her to apologize.

Secretary exits.

MAGGIE: I'm not going to work tomorrow. *She lies down on the bed as though crushed.*

QUENTIN: Okay.

MAGGIE, *half springing up*: You know it's not "okay"! You're scared to death they'll sue me, why don't you say it?

QUENTIN: I'm not scared to death; it's just that you're so wonderful in this show and it's a pity to—

MAGGIE, *sitting up furiously*: All you care about is money! Don't shit me!

QUENTIN, *quelling a fury, his voice very level*: Maggie, don't use that language with me, will you?

MAGGIE: Call me vulgar, that I talk like a truck driver! Well, that's where I come from. I'm for Negroes and Puerto Ricans and truck drivers!

QUENTIN: Then why do you fire people so easily?

MAGGIE, *her eyes narrowing—she is seeing him anew*: Look. You don't want me. What the hell are you doing here?

Father and Dan enter, above them.

QUENTIN: I live here. And you do too, but you don't know it yet. But you're going to. I—

FATHER: Where's he going? I need him! What are you?

QUENTIN, *not turning to Father*: I'm here, and I stick it, that's what I am. And one day you're going to catch on. Now go to sleep. I'll be back in ten minutes, I'd like to take a walk.

He starts out and she comes to attention.

MAGGIE: Where you going to walk?

QUENTIN: Just around the block. *She watches him carefully.* There's nobody else, kid; I just want to walk.

MAGGIE, *with great suspicion*: 'Kay.

Father and Dan exit.

He goes a few yards, halts, turns to see her taking a pill bottle and unscrewing the top.

QUENTIN, *coming back*: You can't take pills on top of whisky,

· 98 ·

dear. *He has reached for them. She pulls them away, but he grabs them again and puts them in his pocket.* That's how it happened the last time. And it's not going to happen again. Never. I'll be right back.

MAGGIE—*an intoxication weighs on her speech now*: Why you wear those pants? *He turns back to her, knowing what is coming.* I told you the seat is too tight.

QUENTIN: Well, they made them too tight, but I can take a walk in them.

MAGGIE: Fags wear pants like that; I told you. They attract each other with their asses.

QUENTIN: You calling me a fag now?

MAGGIE, *very drunk*: Just I've known fags and some of them didn't even know themselves that they were. . . . And I didn't know if you knew about that.

QUENTIN: That's a hell of a way to reassure yourself, Maggie.

MAGGIE, *staggering slightly*: I'm allowed to say what I see!

QUENTIN: You trying to get me to throw you out? Is that what it is? So life will get real again?

MAGGIE, *pointing at him, at his control*: Wha's that suppose to be, strong and silent? I mean what is it?

She stumbles and falls. He makes no move to pick her up.

QUENTIN, *standing over her*: And now I walk out, huh? And you finally know where you are, huh? *He picks her up angrily.* Is that what you want?

Breaking from him, she pitches forward. He catches her and roughly puts her on the bed.

MAGGIE: Wha's the angle? Whyn't you beat it? *She gets on her feet again.* You gonna wait till I'm old? You know what another cab driver said to me today? "I'll give you fifty dollars . . ." *An open, lost sob, wild and contradictory, flies out of her.* You know what's fifty dollars to a cab driver? *Her pain moves into him, his anger is swamped with it.* Go ahead, you can go; I can even walk a straight line, see? Look, see? *She walks with arms out, one foot in front of the other.* So what is it, heh? I mean you want dancing? You want dancing? *Breathlessly she turns on the phonograph and goes into a hip-flinging caricature of a dance around him.* I mean what do you want? What is it?

QUENTIN: Please don't do that. *He catches her and lays her down on the bed.*

MAGGIE: You gonna wait till I'm old? Or what? I mean what is it? What is it?

She lies there, gasping. He stares down at her, addressing the Listener, as he sits beside the bed.

QUENTIN: It's that if there is love, it must be limitless; a love not even of persons but blind, blind to insult, blind to the spear in the flesh, like justice blind, like . . .

Felice appears behind him. He has been raising up his arms. Father appears, slumped in chair.

MOTHER'S VOICE, *off:* Idiot!

A dozen men appear on second level, under the harsh white light of a subway platform, some of them reading newspapers. Apart from them Mickey and Lou appear from each side, approaching each other.

MAGGIE, *rushing off unsteadily:* I mean whyn't you beat it?

QUENTIN, *his arms down, crying out to Listener:* But in whose name do you turn your back?

MICKEY: That we go together, Lou, and name the names! Lou!

Lou, staring at Quentin, mounts the platform where the men wait for a subway train.

QUENTIN: I saw it clear—in whose name you turn your back! I saw it once, I saw the name!

The approaching sound of a subway train is heard, and Lou leaps; the racking squeal of brakes.

LOU: Quentin! Quentin!

All the men look at Quentin, then at the "tracks." The men groan. Quentin's hands are a vise against his head. The tower lights as . . . Mother enters in prewar costume, sailboat in hand, bending toward the "bathroom door" as before.

QUENTIN: In whose name? In whose blood-covered name do you look into a face you loved, and say, Now you have been found wanting, and now in your extremity you die! It had a name, it . . .

MOTHER, *toward the "bathroon. door"*: Quentin? Quentin?

QUENTIN: Hah? *He hurries toward her, but in fear.*

MOTHER: See what we brought you from Atlantic City! From the boardwalk!

Men exit from subway platform. A tremendous crash of surf spins Quentin about, and Mother is gone and the light of the moon is rising on the pier.

QUENTIN: By the ocean. That cottage. That night. The last night.

Maggie in a rumpled wrapper, a bottle in her hand, her hair in snags over her face, staggers out to the edge of the pier and stands in the sound of the surf. Now she starts to topple over the edge of the pier, and he rushes to her and holds her in his hands. Maggie turns around and they embrace. Now the sound of jazz from within is heard, softly.

MAGGIE: You were loved, Quentin; no man was ever loved like you.

QUENTIN, *releasing her*: Carrie tell you I called? My plane couldn't take off all day—

MAGGIE, *drunk, but aware:* I was going to kill myself just now. *He is silent.* Or don't you believe that either?

QUENTIN, *with an absolute calm, a distance, but without hostility:* I saved you twice, why shouldn't I believe it? *Going toward her:* This dampness is bad for your throat, you oughtn't be out here.

MAGGIE—*she defiantly sits, her legs dangling:* Where've *you* been?

QUENTIN, *going upstage, removing his jacket:* I've been in Chicago. I told you. The Hathaway estate.

MAGGIE, *with a sneer:* Estates!

QUENTIN: Well, I have to pay some of our debts before I save the world. *He removes his jacket and puts it on bureau box; sits and removes a shoe.*

MAGGIE, *from the pier:* Didn't you hear what I told you?

QUENTIN: I heard it. I'm not coming out there, Maggie, it's too wet.

She looks *toward him, gets up, unsteadily enters the room.*

MAGGIE: I didn't go to rehearsal today.

QUENTIN: I didn't think you did.

MAGGIE: And I called the network that I'm not finishing that stupid show. I'm an artist! And I don't have to do stupid shows, no matter what contract you made!

QUENTIN: I'm very tired, Maggie. I'll sleep in the living room. Good night. *He stands and starts out upstage.*

MAGGIE: What *is* this?

Pause. *He turns back to her from the exit.*

QUENTIN: I've been fired.

MAGGIE: You're not fired.

QUENTIN: I didn't expect you to take it seriously, but it is to me; I can't make a decision any more without something sits up inside me and busts out laughing.

MAGGIE: That my fault, huh?

Slight pause. Then he resolves.

QUENTIN: Look, dear, it's gone way past blame or justifying ourselves, I . . . talked to your doctor this afternoon.

MAGGIE, *stiffening with fear and suspicion*: About what?

QUENTIN: You want to die, Maggie, and I really don't know how to prevent it. But it struck me that I have been playing with your life out of some idiotic hope of some kind that you'd come out of this endless spell. But there's only one hope, dear—you've got to start to look at what *you're* doing.

MAGGIE: You going to put me away somewhere. Is that it?

QUENTIN: Your doctor's trying to get a plane up here tonight; you settle it with him.

MAGGIE: You're not going to put *me* anywhere, mister. *She opens the pill bottle.*

QUENTIN: You have to be supervised, Maggie. *She swallows pills.* Now listen to me while you can still hear. If you start going under tonight I'm calling the ambulance. I haven't the strength to go through that alone again. I'm not protecting you from the newspapers any more, Maggie, and the hospital means a headline. *She raises the whisky bottle to drink.* You've got to start facing the consequences of your actions, Maggie. *She drinks whisky.* Okay. I'll tell Carrie to call the ambulance as soon as she sees the signs. I'm going to sleep at the inn. *He gets his jacket.*

MAGGIE: Don't sleep at the inn!

QUENTIN: Then put that stuff away and go to sleep.

MAGGIE—*afraid he is leaving, she tries to smooth her tangled hair*: Could you . . . stay five minutes?

QUENTIN: Yes. *He returns.*

MAGGIE: You can even have the bottle if you want. I won't take any more. *She puts the pill bottle on the bed before him.*

QUENTIN, *against his wish to take it*: I don't want the bottle.

MAGGIE: 'Member how used talk to me till I fell asleep?

QUENTIN: Maggie, I've sat beside you in darkened rooms for days and weeks at a time, and my office looking high and low for me—

MAGGIE: No, you lost patience with me.

QUENTIN, *after a slight pause*: That's right, yes.

MAGGIE: So you lied, right?

QUENTIN: Yes, I lied. Every day. We are all separate people. I tried not to be, but finally one is—a separate person. I have to survive too, honey.

MAGGIE: So where you going to put me?

QUENTIN, *trying not to break*: You discuss that with your doctor.

MAGGIE: But if you loved me . . .

QUENTIN: But how would you know, Maggie? Do you know any more who I am? Aside from my name? I'm all the evil in the world, aren't I? All the betrayal, the broken hopes, the murderous revenge? *She pours pills into her hand, and he stands. Now fear is in his voice. A suicide kills two people, Maggie, that's what it's for! So I'm removing myself, and perhaps it will lose its point. He resolutely starts out. She falls back on the bed. Her breathing is suddenly deep. He starts toward Carrie, who sits in semi-darkness, praying.* Carrie!

MAGGIE: Quentin, what's Lazarus?

· 104 ·

He halts. She looks about for him, not knowing he has left.

Quentin?

Not seeing him, she starts up off the bed; a certain alarm . . .

Quen?

He comes halfway back.

QUENTIN: Jesus raised him from the dead. In the Bible. Go to sleep now.

MAGGIE: Wha's 'at suppose to prove?

QUENTIN: The power of faith.

MAGGIE: What about those who have no faith?

QUENTIN: They only have the will.

MAGGIE: But how you get the will?

QUENTIN: You have faith.

MAGGIE: Some apples. *She lies back. A pause.* I want more cream puffs. And my birthday dress? If I'm good? Mama? I want my mother! *She sits up, looks about as in a dream, turns and sees him.* Why you standing there? *She gets out of bed, squinting, and comes up to him, peers into his face; her expression comes alive.* You—you want music?

QUENTIN: All right, you lie down, and I'll put a little music on.

MAGGIE: No, you; you, sit down. And take off your shoes. I mean just to rest. You don't have to do anything. *She staggers to the machine, turns it on; jazz. She tries to sing, but suddenly comes totally awake.* Was I sleeping?

QUENTIN: For a moment, I think.

MAGGIE, *coming toward him in terror*: Was—was my—was anybody else here?

QUENTIN: No. Just me.

MAGGIE: Is there smoke? *With a cry she clings to him; he holds her close.*

QUENTIN: Your mother's dead and gone, dear, she can't hurt you any more, don't be afraid.

MAGGIE, *in the helpless voice of a child as he returns her to the bed*: Where you going to put me?

QUENTIN, *his chest threatening a sob*: Nowhere, dear—the doctor'll decide with you.

MAGGIE: See? I'll lay down. *She lies down.* See? *She takes a strange, deep breath.* You—you could have the pills if you want.

QUENTIN—*stands and, after a hesitation, starts away*: I'll have Carrie come in and take them.

MAGGIE, *sliding off the bed, holding the pill bottle out to him*: No. I won't give them to Carrie. Only you. You take them.

QUENTIN: Why do you want me to have them?

MAGGIE, *extending them*: Here.

QUENTIN, *after a pause*: Do you see it, Maggie? Right now? You're trying to make me the one who does it to you? I grab them; and then we fight, and then I give them up, and you take your death from me. Something in you has been setting me up for a murder. Do you see it? *He moves backward.* But now I'm going away; so you're not my victim any more. It's just you, and your hand.

MAGGIE: But Jesus must have loved her.

QUENTIN: Who?

MAGGIE: Lazarus?

Pause. He sees, he gropes toward his vision.

QUENTIN: That's right, yes! He . . . loved her enough to raise her from the dead. But He's God, see . . . and God's power is love without limit. But when a man dares reach for that . . . he is only reaching for the power. Whoever goes to save another person with the lie of limitless love throws a shadow on the face of God. And God is what happened, God is what is; and whoever stands between another person and her truth is not a lover, he is . . . *He breaks off, lost, peering, and turns back to Maggie for his clue*. And then she said. *He goes back to Maggie, crying out to invoke her*. And then she said!

MAGGIE: I still hear you. Way inside. Quentin? My love? I hear you! Tell me what happened!

QUENTIN, *through a sudden burst of tears*: Maggie, we . . . used one another!

MAGGIE: Not me, not me!

QUENTIN: Yes, you. And I. "To live" we cried, and "Now" we cried. And loved each other's innocence, as though to love enough what was not there would cover up what was. But there is an angel, and night and day he brings back to us exactly what we want to lose. So you must love him because he keeps truth in the world. You eat those pills to blind yourself, but if you could only say, "I have been cruel," this frightening room would open. If you could say, "I have been kicked around, but I have been just as inexcusably vicious to others, called my husband idiot in public, I have been utterly selfish despite my generosity, I have been hurt by a long line of men but I have cooperated with my persecutors—"

MAGGIE—*she has been writhing in fury*: Son of a bitch!

QUENTIN: "And I am full of hatred; I, Maggie, sweet lover of all life—I hate the world!"

MAGGIE: Get out of here!

QUENTIN: Hate women, hate men, hate all who will not grovel at my feet proclaiming my limitless love for ever and ever! But no pill can make us innocent. Throw them in the sea, throw death in the sea and all your innocence. Do the hardest thing of all—see your own hatred and live!

MAGGIE: What about your hatred? You know when I wanted to die. When I read what you wrote, kiddo. Two months after we were married, kiddo.

QUENTIN: Let's keep it true—you told me you tried to die long before you met me.

MAGGIE: So you're not even there, huh? I didn't even meet you. You coward! What about your hatred! *She moves front.* I was married to a king, you son of a bitch! I was looking for a fountain pen to sign some autographs. And there's his desk—*She is speaking toward some invisible source of justice now, telling her injury*—and there's his empty chair where he sits and thinks how to help people. And there's his handwriting. And there's some words. *She almost literally reads in the air, and with the same original astonishment.* "The only one I will ever love is my daughter. If I could only find an honorable way to die." *Now she turns to him.* When you gonna face that, Judgey? Remember how I fell down, fainted? On the new rug? That's what killed me, Judgey. Right? *She staggers up to him, and into his face:* 'Zat right?

QUENTIN, *after a pause:* All right. You pour them back, and I'll tell you the truth about that.

MAGGIE: You won't tell truth.

> *He tries to tip her hand toward the bottle, holding both her wrists.*

QUENTIN, *with difficulty:* We'll see. Pour them back first, and we'll see.

> *She lets him pour them back, but sits on the bed, holding the bottle in both hands.*

MAGGIE, *after a deep breath:* Liar.

QUENTIN, *in quiet tension against his own self-condemnation*: We'd had our first party in our own house. Some important people, network heads, directors—

MAGGIE: And you were ashamed of me. Don't lie, now! You're still playing God! That's what killed me, Quentin!

QUENTIN: All right. I wasn't . . . ashamed. But . . . afraid. *Pause.* I wasn't sure if any of them . . . had had you.

MAGGIE, *astounded*: But I didn't know any of those!

QUENTIN, *not looking at her*: I swear to you, I did get to where I couldn't imagine what I'd ever been ashamed of. But it was too late. I had written that, and I was like all the others who'd betrayed you, and I could never be trusted again.

MAGGIE, *with a mixture of accusation and lament for a lost life, weeping*: Why did you write that?

QUENTIN: Because when the guests had gone, and you suddenly turned on me, calling me cold, remote, it was the first time I saw your eyes that way—betrayed, screaming that I'd made you feel you didn't exist—

MAGGIE: Don't mix me up with Louise!

QUENTIN: That's just it. That I could have brought two women so different to the same accusation—it closed a circle for me. And I wanted to face the worst thing I could imagine—that I could not love. And I wrote it down, like a letter from hell.

She starts to raise her hand to her mouth, and he steps in and holds her wrist.

That's rock bottom. What more do you *want*?

She looks at him; her eyes unreadable.

Maggie, we were both born of many errors; a human being has to forgive himself! Neither of us is innocent. What more do you want?

A strange calm overtakes her. She lies back on the bed. The hostility seems to have gone.

MAGGIE: Love me, and do what I tell you. And stop arguing. *He moves in anguish up and down beside the bed.* And take down the sand dune. It's *not* too expensive. I want to hear the ocean when we make love in here, but we never hear the ocean.

QUENTIN: We're nearly broke, Maggie; and that dune keeps the roof from blowing off.

MAGGIE: So you buy a new roof. I'm cold. Lie on me.

QUENTIN: I can't do that again, not when you're like this.

MAGGIE: Just till I sleep!

QUENTIN—*an outcry*: Maggie, it's a mockery. Leave me *something*.

MAGGIE: Just out of humanness! I'm cold!

Holding down self-disgust, he lies down on her but holds his head away. Pause.

If you don't argue with me any more, I'll let you be my lawyer again. 'Kay? If you don't argue? Ludwig doesn't argue. *He is silent.* And don't keep saying we're broke? And the sand dune? *The agony is growing in his face, of total disintegration.* 'Cause I love the ocean sound; like a big mother—sssh, sssh, sssh. *He lifts himself off, stands looking down at her. Her eyes are closed.* You gonna be good now? *She takes a very deep breath.*

He reaches in carefully and tries to snatch the bottle; she grips it.

QUENTIN: It isn't my love you want any more. It's my destruction! But you're not going to kill me, Maggie. I want those pills. I don't want to fight you, Maggie. Now put them in my hand.

She looks at him, then quickly tries to swallow her handful, but he knocks some of them out—although she swallows

many. He grabs for the bottle, but she holds and he pulls,
yanks. She goes with the force, and he drags her onto the
floor, trying to pry her hands open as she flails at him and hits
his face—her strength is wild and no longer her own. He
grabs her wrist and squeezes it with both his fists.

Drop them, you bitch! You won't kill me!

She holds on, and suddenly, clearly, he lunges for her throat
and lifts her with his grip.

You won't kill me! You won't kill me!

She drops the bottle as from the farthest distance Mother
rushes to the "bathroom door," crying out—the toy sailboat
in her hand.

MOTHER: Darling, open this door! I didn't trick you!

Quentin springs away from Maggie, who falls back to the
floor, his hands open and in air.

Mother continues without halt.

Quentin, why are you running water in there! *She backs away in*
horror from the "door." I'll die if you do that! I saw a star when
you were born—a light, a light in the world.

He stands transfixed as Mother backs into his hand, which
of its own volition, begins to squeeze her throat. She sinks
to the floor, gasping for breath. And he falls back in horror.

QUENTIN: Murder?

Maggie gets to her hands and knees, gasping. He rushes to
help her, terrified by his realization. She flails out at him, and
on one elbow looks up at him in a caricature of laughter, her
eyes victorious and wild with fear.

MAGGIE: Now we both know. You tried to kill me, mister. I been
killed by a lot of people, some couldn't hardly spell, but it's the
same, mister. You're on the end of a long, long line, Frank.

As though to ward off the accusation, he reaches again to help her up, and in absolute terror she springs away across the floor.

Stay 'way! . . . No! No—no, Frank. Don't you do that. *Cautiously, as though facing a wild, ravening beast:* Don't you do that. . . . I'll call Quentin if you do that. *She glances off and calls quietly, but never leaving him out of her sight.* Quentin! Qu—

She falls asleep, crumpled on the floor. Now deep, strange breathing. He .quickly goes to her, throws her over onto her stomach for artificial respiration, but just as he is about to start, he stands. He calls upstage.

QUENTIN: Carrie? Carrie! *Carrie enters. As though it were a final farewell:* Quick! Call the ambulance! Stop wasting time! Call the ambulance!

Carrie exits. He looks down at Maggie, addressing Listener.

No-no, we saved her. It was just in time. Her doctor tells me she had a few good months; he even thought for a while she was making it. Unless, God knows, he fell in love with her too. *He almost smiles; it is gone. He moves out on the dock.* Look, I'll say it. It's really all I came to say. Barbiturates kill by suffocation. And the signal is a kind of sighing—the diaphragm is paralyzed. And I stood out on that dock. *He looks up.* And all those stars, still so fixed, so fortunate! And her precious seconds squirming in my hand, alive as bugs; and I heard. Those deep, unnatural breaths, like the footfalls of my coming peace—and knew . . . I wanted them. How is that possible? I loved that girl!

Enter Lou, Mickey, Father, Dan, Carrie, and Felice at various points. Louise appears.

And the name—yes, the name! In whose name do you ever turn your back—*He looks out at the audience*—but in your own? In Quentin's name. Always in your own blood-covered name you turn your back!

Holga appears on the highest level.

HOLGA: But no one is innocent they did not kill!

QUENTIN: But love, is love enough? What love, what wave of pity will ever reach this knowledge—I know how to kill? . . . I know, I know—she was doomed in any case, but will that cure? Or is it possible—*He turns toward the tower, moves toward it as toward a terrible God*—that this is not bizarre . . . to anyone? And I am not alone, and no man lives who would not rather be the sole survivor of this place than all its finest victims! What is the cure? Who can be innocent again on this mountain of skulls? I tell you what I know! My brothers died here—*He looks from the tower down at the fallen Maggie*—but my brothers built this place; our hearts have cut these stones! And what's the cure? . . . No, not love; I loved them all, all! And gave them willing to failure and to death that I might live, as they gave me and gave each other, with a word, a look, a trick, a truth, a lie—and all in love!

HOLGA: Hello!

QUENTIN: But what will defend her? *He cries up to Holga*: That woman hopes!

She stands unperturbed, resolute, aware of his pain and her own.

Or is that—*Struck, to the Listener*—exactly why she hopes, because she knows? What burning cities taught her and the death of love taught me: that we are very dangerous! *Staring, seeing his vision*: And that, that's why I wake each morning like a boy—even now, even now! I swear to you, I could love the world again! Is the knowing all? To know, and even happily, that we meet unblessed; not in some garden of wax fruit and painted trees, that lie of Eden, but after, after the Fall, after many, many deaths. Is the knowing all? And the wish to kill is never killed, but with some gift of courage one may look into its face when it appears, and with a stroke of love—as to an idiot in the house—forgive it; again and again . . . forever?

He is evidently interrupted by the Listener.

No, it's not certainty, I don't feel that. But it does seem feasible . . . not to be afraid. Perhaps it's all one has. I'll tell her that. . . . Yes, she will, she'll know what I mean.

He turns upstage. He hesitates; all his people face him. He walks toward Louise, pausing; but she turns her face away. He goes on and pauses beside Mother, who stands in uncomprehending sorrow; he gestures as though he touched her, and she looks up at him and dares a smile, and he smiles back. He pauses at his dejected Father and Dan, and with a slight gesture magically makes them stand. Felice is about to raise her hand in blessing—he shakes her hand, aborting her enslavement. He passes Mickey and Lou and turns back to Maggie; she rises from the floor, webbed in with her demons, trying to awake. And with his life following him he climbs toward Holga, who raises her arm as though seeing him, and with great love . . .

HOLGA: Hello!

He comes to a halt a few yards from her and walks toward her, holding out his hand.

QUENTIN: Hello.

He moves away with her as a loud whispering comes up from all his people, who follow behind, endlessly alive. Darkness takes them all.

The play was directed by Elia Kazan and produced by Robert Whitehead for the Lincoln Center Repertory Company. It was first performed on January 23, 1964, at the ANTA–Washington Square Theatre, New York City.

THE CAST
(In order of appearance)

QUENTIN	JASON ROBARDS, JR.
FELICE	ZOHRA LAMPERT
MAGGIE	BARBARA LODEN
HOLGA	SALOME JENS
DAN	MICHAEL STRONG
FATHER	PAUL MANN
MOTHER	VIRGINIA KAYE
NURSES	FAYE DUNAWAY, DIANE SHALET
ELSIE	PATRICIA ROE
LOUISE	MARICLARE COSTELLO
LOU	DAVID J. STEWART
MICKEY	RALPH MEEKER
MAN IN PARK	STANLEY BECK
CARRIE	RUTH ATTAWAY
LUCAS	HAROLD SCOTT
CHAIRMAN	DAVID WAYNE
HARLEY BARNES	HAL HOLBROOK
PORTER	JACK WALTZER
MAGGIE'S SECRETARY	CRYSTAL FIELD
PIANIST	SCOTT CUNNINGHAM
OTHERS	CLINT KIMBROUGH, JOHN PHILLIP LAW,
	BARRY PRIMUS, JAMES GREENE

ELSIE .... Patricia Fox

LOU .... David Stewart